Around & A

THE HALDO.

– *Revisited*

Chips Barber

**assisted by
Sally Barber**

*To John
all the very best!
Chips Barber.*

OBELISK PUBLICATIONS

ALSO BY THE AUTHOR

The Lost City of Exeter
Diary of a Dartmoor Walker
The Torbay Book*
Diary of a Devonshire Walker
The Great Little Dartmoor Book
The Great Little Exeter Book
DevonAir Book of Family Walks*
Made in Devon
Dartmoor in Colour*
Burgh Island and Bigbury Bay
Dark & Dastardly Dartmoor
Exeter in Colour*
Torbay in Colour
Ghosts of Exeter
The Great Little Totnes Book
Tales of the Teign
Ten Family Walks on Dartmoor
The Great Little Plymouth Book
Plymouth in Colour
Weird & Wonderful Dartmoor
Ghastly & Ghostly Devon
Dawlish and Dawlish Warren

The South Hams
Torquay / Paignton / Brixham
Ten Family Walks in East Devon
Around & About Salcombe
Around & About Seaton
Around & About Sidmouth
Around & About Teignmouth and Shaldon
Chudleigh Collection
Brixham Album
Topsham Past and Present
Beautiful Dartmoor
From The Dart to The Start
Dartmouth and Kingswear
Cranmere Pool – The First Dartmoor Letterbox
The Great Little Chagford Book
The Teign Valley of Yesteryear Parts I and II
Brixham of Yesteryear Parts I, II, III
Pinhoe of Yesteryear Parts I and II
Haunted Pubs in Devon
Princetown of Yesteryear Parts I and II
The South Hams in Colour
Six Short Pub Walks on Dartmoor

*titles no longer available

This book is dedicated to Andrea, Jenna and Jimmy

Acknowledgments

Many thanks are due to everybody who helped in the preparation of both the original version and revised edition of this book. In addition to everyone mentioned by name within the following pages, I must thank Dave Barrett for his photographs, Jane Reynolds for her drawings, Dave Whalley for his diagram, Nicholas Toyne for the inside photos of Smokey Joe, Michael Williams for his cover photo of Smokey Joe, Phil Chambers, John Hunt, Mr Merton, Babs Creed, Steve Coombes, Tim Legood, William Burkinshaw, Colin Burges, the late H.R. Rivers and Dr Ian Goodrick. Also the Forestry Commission, the Express & Echo and the Westcountry Studies Library, Exeter (part of Devon Library Services).

First published in 1982 (0 946651 14 0), Reprinted in 1983, 1986 and 1988
Revised edition (1 899073 31 0) published in 1996 by
Obelisk Publications, 2 Church Hill, Pinhoe, Exeter, Devon
Designed by Chips and Sally Barber
Printed in Great Britain by

CONTENTS

INTRODUCTION

The original version of this book was first published in 1982 and was for me, working together with my wife, a first tentative step into the world of publishing. Since then we have made great strides and published well over a hundred books on a variety of Devonshire topics, which include walking, ghosts, nostalgia, specific places and so on. Happily, the demand for this book goes on but since 1982 many things have also moved on apace, and the Haldon Hills have witnessed many changes. Therefore we feel the time is right to present a new, revised and amended book.

These hills are the hidden hill range of Devon, despite being seen from almost every vantage point in the county. They are hidden in the sense that periodicals and books seem to possess a blind spot when it comes to writing about them; Dartmoor, Exmoor, yes – but the Haldons seem to have been forgotten many times.

It is mainly for this reason that I first set out on this Devonian safari in an attempt to put into words, photos, maps and diagrams what these 'Cinderella Hills' are all about. Where shelves full of Dartmoor and Exmoor books seem to multiply with each new season, the Haldons remain in the shadows of their loftier relations.

To me the challenge is to tell the stories of the Haldons and surrounding districts in a way which will entertain you and enrich your knowledge about a part of Devon for too long undiscovered.

This is a story of people. It tells of vagabonds in the hedgerows and of Barons in exceedingly wealthy homes. There is a story that Sunday newspapers would bid highly for, if it were not from two centuries ago. There are a few Irish stories, funny but sadly true.

It is also the story of the unusual, from massive swans to orange elephants, and from headless hermits to murdering monks. It is a land where treacle oozes from the ground and where if you visit a particular pub, you might well find 'nobody in'.

If you are perplexed by any of these ideas, do not worry, all will be revealed! The Haldon Hills have a magnetism, which attracts the whole spectrum of people. However, many people still pass by unsuspectingly along fast highways. Come with me to see what they are missing ...

HALDON — THE BARRIER

The Haldon Hills form a formidable tract of upland south of Exeter, generally flat on top but flanked by impressive slopes and deep combes on all sides. Although not so high or so wild as Dartmoor, from which it is separated by the valley of the River Teign, Haldon has a distinctive character of its own, one that has been reflected in the people who have lived and worked – or, in some cases, lived without working – on it over many centuries.

The Haldon Hills owe their origin to a near-horizontal layer of sandstone and flint that formed part of a once more-extensive layer that stretched from the fringe of Dartmoor eastward into Dorset and beyond. Rivers cut valleys across this layer, forming the valleys of the Exe, Teign and smaller streams, but Haldon was left standing, despite the many combes eroded into its sides. These combes account for the ragged outline of the hills on a map and, indeed, for the break in the plateau at Rixdale that separates Great Haldon and Little Haldon. They also give the slopes a quite different character to the plateau: the latter is dominated by heath land and forest, the former characterised by farmsteads and small villages tucked away in folds of land where the twentieth century seems to have caused little change. The farmland stretches away to the coastline and Teign estuary, where a 'tourist landscape', of chalets and caravans, has appeared, at least in part; but the great majority of Haldon's slopes remain unaffected, uniquely charming and pleasantly peaceful.

The Railway Builders

The highest point on Haldon is 817 feet (249 m) above sea level, and much of the plateau is above 700 feet (213 m). Nowhere can it be crossed without rising to at least 570 feet (174 m), and this fact has been an influence on the routes people have taken from Exeter southwards. This range of hills was a consideration of the various nineteenth century railway engineers, including the great Isambard Kingdom Brunel, when trying to forge routes westward. Although it was feasible to forge a straighter route between Exeter and Newton Abbot, this more direct route didn't materialise. Instead the main line opted for the lowland route to embrace as many settlements as possible and the other more northerly route, between Exeter and Newton, became the Teign Valley line. Many pictures of it in its hey-day are featured in my books *The Teign Valley of Yesteryear* parts one and two.

Many years ago, one autumn day, with two friends, I traced part of the section of railway near Longdown. Weighed down with tripods and other photographic equipment we explored land which is private, having gained the kind permission of Mrs Eden of Culver, beforehand. In one of the tunnels there appeared to be a mushroom farm of some note. The very damp conditions must have been ideal for such an unusually sited activity.

That day we found, to our great surprise, Longdown Station, well away from the village and situated between the Perridge and Culver tunnels. Thinking it to be in an excellent state of preservation considering the twenty-plus years it had been closed, we later learnt that this wasn't the hand of nature being benign but the tender, loving care of railwayman Colin Burges. Prior to this remedial work, vandals had been at work in the early 1960s, Longdown station having been needlessly wrecked. A restoration project between 1975-1978 had brought the station back towards resembling its former self, with even the addition of new signs and a map.

Undoubtedly this line of ineffable, sylvan beauty would surely have been a great tourist attraction had it survived the era of branch line closures in the late 1950s. This was still several years before 'The Beeching Axe', which fell in 1963 to further shrink the rail network.

The problem with the Teign Valley line was that the railway followed a lowland route, where possible, whereas most of its potential passengers lived high up on the valley sides, unlike the Exe Valley line, which served its settlements closer to the valley floor.

Before the line was ever opened it was a controversial scheme, needing no less than seven Acts of Parliament to be passed before finally being engineered.

The lower section of the line, from Newton Abbot to Ashton, had opened in 1882 owing to the effort of Lord Chudleigh but it was not completed until 1 July 1903.

The Teign Valley railway entertained Royal Trains from time to time, and was more than useful when the main line coastal route, through Dawlish, was closed for various reasons, like storm or landslip. It is well known that the Cornish Riviera Express was diverted along it on occasions but even this great express train had to proceed at a much reduced speed of about thirty miles per hour.

Dennis Luxton, a train driver on this former branch line, has many fond memories of working on this line in the days of steam. Those who romanticise at the 'Golden Age' of steam should appreciate some of the predicaments which arose.

From time to time engines would grind to a halt in a tunnel, either Perridge or

Culver tunnels. In order to get the train mobile again Dennis or his contemporaries would be forced to alight. An atmosphere filled with sulphurous steam and the incessant dripping from the tunnel ceiling forced the driver to wrap his coat around his face to avoid asphyxiation. On these occasions sand would be shovelled onto the rails so that the locomotive could grip sufficiently to get moving. In such circumstances everything would be coloured with a yellowish-green tinge, including the driver.

Another problem on cold mornings centred around the steam engine's thirst for some fourteen hundred gallons of water in order to make sufficient steam. It seems that an initial tank load would enable the train to get from Exeter to Heathfield and then back to Christow. Cold mornings would freeze the supply and when the ice could not be broken it was either a case of 'fingers crossed' back to Exeter, or all available hands to the nearest tap carrying two-gallon buckets. Filling a fourteen hundred gallon tank was far from easy; on one occasion slopping buckets gave a coating of ice on the platform at Christow. The engine driver, in his endeavours to keep 'God's Wonderful Railway' to time, shot off the end of the platform — to the great amusement of the passengers (once they realised that he was not hurt).

Timetables on this line were more of a general guideline. Dennis Luxton described the route as a 'Tin Pot Railway' which used geriatric or novice engine drivers, and all sorts of unusual practices were evident.

The line suited many of the staff as it gave them the opportunity to practise their 'cuisine'. Lard and butcher's bacon would be taken on a journey and these would be expertly cooked in the locomotive's fiery furnace, being placed on the fireman's shovel. At the right time of the year the drivers and station staff would use the mushrooms grown in the fields beside the line for more feasting.

During the last war ambulance trains operated over the Teign Valley Branch as far as Chudleigh, where temporary platforms/ramps were built. Casualties were taken to the US hospital at Stover, which later became the Polish refugee camp. The Manor House Hotel (GR Hotels) at Moretonhampstead was used as a hospital, but it is not known how this was served. The carriages were kept sterile with the drivers barred from entry. One signalman stationed at Longdown during the War believed that ambulance trains used to offload there, but this does not make sense – unless they were casualties for Moreton. He also recalled Frank Whittle, designer of the jet engine, who was resident at Culver during the Second World War, often taking his daily 'constitutional' to the station.

The line saw plenty of industrial use, but most passengers living in the remote villages of Trusham, Ashton and Doddiscombsleigh, in the post-war years, opted for the independence of the motor car. Some of these villages petitioned against the closure but, as always, economics won the day; the last train passed along the line in 1958.

Many of the stations have since been converted to private dwellings. At Christow Station, which is closer to Doddiscombsleigh, the station building has been adapted as a residence. The weather vane depicts a steam engine and the platforms have been attractively landscaped. However, in part of the goods yard at Christow Station, something of a railway revival has happened in the establishment of a base for the small but ambitious 'Exeter & Teign Valley Railway', privately owned and operated by Colin Burges.

Although much preparatory work had been undertaken, it was really the whistle of a locomotive – this time a small diesel shunter – that announced the return of the railway to Christow after more than 30 years' absence.

Now, abruptly, dereliction borders the neatness and order of a railway taking shape; this at a place where some local people do not know that there ever was a train service. Despite the contrast between the work of man and Nature, the railway is remarkably unobtrusive and sits comfortably in its tranquil surroundings; quite unlike the system of transport which finds favour today. Several differences between road and rail are portrayed in blunt style beside the public footpath which crosses the line. The site is not formally open to the public but a small exhibition is available for viewing in the summer, admission being by platform ticket for a modest sum. Rides are sometimes given in a narrow gauge carriage for a contribution to the Southern Railway Homes for Children.

If the railway companies had proved more successful, two other lines might have been linked to the Teign Valley line. One was a branch along the Teign up to Chagford along one of the most splendid valleys in England; the other route considered was to link Crediton with Newton Abbot in a more direct line. This would have passed close to Tedburn St Mary, linking with the Teign Valley line near Leigh Cross. Rail enthusiasts are quick to assert the point that whereas major roads can be a blot on the landscape, the forging of new rail routes had a much less dramatic impact on the landscape.

The history of the main railway line following the South Devon coast, originally pioneered by Brunel using the Atmospheric Railway system, is already well documented in other publications. The failure of Brunel's imaginative system, and the subsequent £375,000 losses, was illustrated, for many years by the semi-derelict appearance of the Starcross Pumping House. However it did become 'The Brunel Atmospheric Railway', a museum to relate how the system worked. There was even a working model, powered by a vacuum cleaner, that demonstrated the atmospheric principle admirably. This has since closed.

For several years a pub in Starcross, called 'The Atmospheric Railway', has had Brunel on its inn sign. Prior to this an illustration of the Pumping House, and the broad gauge railway lines with the pipe laid between them, did the job and also gave a history lesson at the same time.

The threat that the sea poses between Dawlish Warren and Teignmouth is a real one, particularly when the equinoctial storms rage around this coastline. One of the few facts rarely recorded about the tunnelled section between those stations is that it provided the setting for a book written in the early part of this century, by Maurice Drake, an Exeter watch maker, strangely entitled '*WO₂*'. He used one of the tunnels to portray a gold bullion robbery. It seems that a sea cave running into the drains of the tunnel allowed access for the Plymouth Boat Train to be robbed. I have looked for a copy of it in countless second hand and antiquarian bookshops, over a period of many years, but all to no avail. Maurice's masterpiece may probably be worth as much as the gold bullion that he wrote about!

Parson and Clerk

Close to the railway is a sea stack called 'The Parson and Clerk' which has prompted a multitude of story interpretations as to its origin. The one I choose to convey involves Haldon, providing another link with the hills.

A parson and a clerk of Dawlish had visited the Bishop of Exeter who was apparently on his death bed. It was not the Bishop's health that was the parson's true concern, but the possibility of succeeding him that prompted the journey. They passed over Haldon Moors on the return journey, with the customary poor weather evident on its lofty summit. So atrocious were the conditions that the parson cursed the clerk, saying that he would have preferred the Devil as his guide. Whereupon, the Haldon scenery blazed with bright lights and the revelry of jovial music welcomed them to a newly sited inn of immense dimensions. Ensconced within, the pair enjoyed a riotous time but, as day dawned, the dream palace disappeared leaving both of them petrified in the sea off Holcombe Head. The 'Parson and Clerk' stories vary greatly. This is but one of many sagas illustrating the folly of wishing ill on fellow beings and getting involved in a relationship with the Devil.

Flying

In the past the upland plateau of Little Haldon provided a useful tableland for another form of transport. Some most unusual happenings have occurred on and above the fairways of Teignmouth's elevated golf course. I wonder if the golfers ever spare a thought for the other objects, other than golf balls, which once flew over the same space and often as inaccurately – aeroplanes!

Way back in 1929, a windsock proudly streamed outwards from a tall flagpole. On it was the inviting message: 'Learn to Fly at Haldon Aerodrome.' From some accounts, it may have been more appropriate to have substituted the word 'crash' for 'fly', as scares were frequent, with sudden unpredictable gusts of wind buffeting these frail and inconsistent flying machines.

The aerodrome had a short life, but enjoyed many interesting happenings. It also proved to be a launch-pad for several aviators destined for global acclaim. The airfield was opened in 1929 and on 29 September an air rally took place. Many personalities of that era were present, the most notable being the Director of Civil Aviation, Sir Sefton Brancker. But the weather was unduly bad and strong winds whipped up great clouds of dust covering the spectators from head to toe!

Some of the de Havilland Moths were grounded, but a certain Mr Lawson could not be deterred with his autogyro. Gallantly, he won over the crowd with his aerobatics and, amid much applause, landed totally intact. Ironically, after propping up his machine a great gust of wind blew it over and did so much damage that it never flew again. Such are the twists of fate that a few days later, Mr Lawson received a certificate of airworthiness for it.

A 17-year-old pilot stole the show in 1931, flying solo with style and precision. Whitney Straight, not a geographical location but his name, soared to dizzy heights both on the ground and in the air. He formed a chain of flying clubs and pre-war airlines. Eventually he became managing director of BOAC.

At the rallies, a popular event was the Teignmouth Air Race, which was always keenly contested. The trophies are still housed in the council offices at Teignmouth.

If these activities added spice to the small Haldon aerodrome, it was the bread and butter flights which kept it on the map. In 1933 the Great Western Railway showed their continuing enterprise by purchasing an aeroplane from Imperial Airways. The three-engined four-seater Westland Wessex was painted in the familiar livery of the GWR. The inside was fitted in the style of one of their railway carriages.

On 11 April 1933, a twice-daily triangular service operated between Plymouth, Teignmouth and Cardiff. The full return fare from Plymouth to Cardiff was £6, but Teignmouth to Cardiff was

A pilot's eye view of Little Haldon, looking towards the Teign Estuary

£5. Cardiff took about 55 minutes to reach, depending on wind strength and direction. The Teignmouth-Plymouth section took about 25 minutes, with a scenic route being followed along the southern edge of Dartmoor. The pilot for the railway air service was Captain Olley, who eventually formed Olley Air Services, which were well known and respected in the 1930s.

Changeovers were rapid and the GWR sold out to Railway Air Services in 1934 which, with a suggestion of high-flying trains, sounded highly dangerous! Their reign lasted until 1937 when Mr Straight appeared on 1st January of that year with The Straight Corporation taking over. Provincial Airways ran a service with landing stages at Croydon, Portsmouth, Christchurch, Haldon and Plymouth.

With the advent of the Second World War, the Little Haldon Aerodrome ceased civil operations, never to open again. It had been beset with problems of dust and poor weather and the buildings soon decayed and disappeared.

During the Second World War it saw plenty of activity. Gordon Taylor, an ex-Royal Navy pilot, made many bumpy landings there. He flew Seafires, which were the Royal Navy's equivalent of the Spitfire.

In a life which saw him globe-trot, in many forms of aircraft, Gordon maintained his link with the Haldon Hills. He had his own airstrip and helicopter pad at Trusham. With his great friend and co-pilot Herbie Plain, he shared a small fixed-wing aircraft that was also based at his private airfield.

Frequently this dynamic duo, who made names for themselves as speedway riders for Exeter in the 1950s, were called upon to use their aerial skills to help out. Typical of their rescues and adventures was the airlift, in the days when air ambulances were far from the norm, of a pregnant lady from Lynton to hospital at Barnstaple. She was so heavy with child that several items had to be discarded before a lift-off was possible.

Other successful missions saw some hair-raising deliveries of emergency supplies to farmers cut off from the outside world by extremes of weather.

At Christmas time Herbie Plain often became Santa and the duo enjoyed bringing happiness to others by 'dropping in', by helicopter, to perform their festive duties.

Herbie Plain and Gordon Taylor radiated a marvellous enthusiasm for matters aviational. Their memories went back many years and it is hoped that this book will help to keep some of those memories alive. Gordon Taylor has passed away since that time and is buried with his wife, who died soon after him, at a graveyard situated beneath the Haldon Hills that he knew so well and under the skies that he loved so much.

In stark contrast, for others, though, it is these hills that rise so sharply up above the surrounding countryside, that have been the cause of their untimely deaths.

There have been, unfortunately, a number of fatal air crashes in the Haldon Hills area. In 1987, an experienced pilot, Peter Cope was killed when his single-engined plane crashed. The following January, Mike Searle, a member of Exeter Flying Club was killed in a crash at Luscombe Hill near Little Haldon, the cause, according to an accident investigator, probably being confusion due to fog.

Another tragedy occurred in April 1993 when another single engine plane crashed at Breckneck Hill, high above Teignmouth. It had been on its way from Jersey when it came down, also in dense fog, close to the Holcombe Down Christian Retirement Home. Three people in the plane, two men and a lady lost their lives.

Driving

Having seen how shy the railways were of the Haldon Hills, the roads, by contrast, have always boldly gone straight over the top. The modern-day turbo-engined traveller will probably climb over the escarpment with consummate ease and at an

A filling station near the top of Telegraph Hill, which has since been rebuilt

alarming speed. This is by courtesy of traffic engineers who have produced the impressive A38 and A380 highways, surpassing for ease of travel any of the former routes over it. Maybe those motorists should give some thought to the more pedestrian-minded routes which attempted to cross the same barrier centuries ago.

Travellers in the Middle Ages had at least five alternative routes to cross from the Exe Valley up onto the open moorlands that existed then. Most of these tracks can still be seen in sections.

The most northerly was known as Ashlake Road, probably used from the ancient British period as it was a sunken road. The section visible today is from near Idestone (SX 876 883) to Ashlake Cross. This was a deliberately used route from the Exe Valley to parts of the Teign Valley near Doddiscombsleigh. The track was four to five feet wide and sunken to a depth of three feet.

The hollow way, which gives its name to Holloway Barton (SX 893 855), started about a quarter of a mile away from this farm, climbing Deers Hill almost straight up to the summit of Haldon. This is an early Saxon route, probably dating back to the seventh century. Its seven feet depth and five feet width indicated use by plenty of through traffic. It is likely that this was a cattle route or drove road with its high sides preventing cattle from straying into the woodlands and pastures on Haldon's lower scarp slope.

A third track is not named on the map but its route is identical to a modern public right of way which rises at the bottom of Telegraph Hill. It climbs in a southwesterly direction to bisect the minor road running across the top of the escarpment, at a point about half way between the top of Haldon and Telegraph Hills. Unlike the other routes it climbed the hill at an angle, providing an easier climb. It was the original way from Kenn to Haldon, only being sunken to a depth of two feet in its middle section. Originally it crossed the land which is now the racecourse before falling into Oxencombe and on towards Chudleigh.

St Andrew's Lane, a fourth route, ran from Berber Hill up to a point below Haldon Chalet and again this is visible in a modern track following a watershed route. It is a very old track five feet deep in places and was intentionally excavated.

Holloway Lane is the last of the old tracks, and raises the most speculation. Theories put forward indicate that it was neither ancient British nor Saxon but engineered as recently as the Mediaeval Period. Unlike the others it is much longer and was metalled with flint and chert. This was unusual for the Haldon area, suggesting that it carried more traffic than other routes of that time.

The route of Holloway Lane begins at a ferry crossing-point on the Exe Estuary opposite Topsham. The latter was an important port, especially after the construction of a weir on the Exe by members of the Courtenay family in 1284 (possibly Isabella de Fortibus). Its trade, usurped from a truncated Port of Exeter, probably had to be distributed to other parts of the port's hinterland. Holloway Lane passed the southern edge of the present day Exminster, climbed Exminster Hill, crossed Babels Bridge on the River Kenn, before curving to climb Haydon Common. At the top of the common it climbed a long spur rising steeply to reach a point on the road one mile south of the top of Telegraph Hill (SX 913 823).

The woodlands near this point are privately owned. Many years ago the owners, who wished to keep out would-be trespassers, resorted to placing a sign bearing a phrase, the gist of which was 'KEEP OUT– DANGER– TARAXACUM'. Students of botany will know that this word means 'dandelions'. The sign later became 'KEEP OUT–ADDERS'. Perhaps 'PRESERVED ANCIENT TRADE ROUTE' ought to have appeared instead. It linked the two main routes between Exeter and South Devon.

Another frequently-used old trackway between the Exe Valley and Teign Bridge was called 'Gappah' or the Goat's Path. A farmhouse south of Chudleigh still bears this name. The route shows widely spaced hedges over much of its length to this day, evidence that it was once a drove road for conveyance of cattle to market, eventually to London in some cases. The route passes along the watershed above the valleys of Harcombe and Grammarcombe having climbed along a ridge between Ugbrooke Park and the town of Chudleigh, passing Castle Dyke, an Iron Age encampment. From there to Thorns Cross was particularly dangerous, as it was slippery; part of the track lies within the forest, the modern roads taking less hazardous routes, but north of Thorns Cross the width of the old route is readily appreciable on the present A380 trunk road. Waddon, now a few houses only, was once a much more important hamlet in the route's heyday. The route follows the Haldon ridge to its northern extremity where, beside the prominent landmark Lawrence Castle (Haldon Belvedere), an Iron Age encampment was excavated in 1935. Perhaps the route was first cut by those Iron Age inhabitants, the first dwellers on Haldon, giving access to Castle Dyke and other sites. From Lawrence Castle roads descend to Ide and Longdown, the former also showing signs of having been a drove road.

The Turnpike Trust set up in 1750 by Act of Parliament soon began to improve roads. Pack-horse trains and only occasional wheeled vehicles plied their way laboriously across the Haldons. The main route to Chudleigh left Exeter near Alphington Church, passed through Shillingford and crossed over Haldon at Bullers Hill before dropping into Chudleigh. This route is still metalled today and provides a more direct link between these two villages than the drove route; in Alphington it still bears the name Chudleigh Road. Although on some maps it is marked 'Roman Road', there is no evidence that it was built by the Romans; part of it may have been a more ancient route, however, linking Haldon to a ford on the Exe at Salmon Pool through Clapperbrook Lane.

The route over Telegraph Hill existed but not that of Haldon Hill which came into existence in 1822 when Macadam's roads were making vast improvements to the coaching network. Until the 1870s it was a toll road, and the Toll House is still to be seen on the winding section of road that was bypassed in the 1960s by the present trunk road.

The A379, the road by-passing Exminster, but still struggling through Starcross and Dawlish, was first engineered as a route in 1774, providing access to the Teignmouth area without recourse to crossing the Haldon Hills.

Another ancient trade route, probably pre-Roman, was a Port Way which can be traced from Hackney Marshes near Kingsteignton, to Cockwood on the Exe Estuary. As 'port' means to carry it is likely that pack-horses or porters carried goods along this route. The origin and destination points of this route are uncertain. The fishing village of Tormo Hun (now Torquay) was several miles distant and may have been connected. Likewise, Milber Down Camp was a significant Roman site. Both may have used the long established ferry crossing place, near the present A380 road bridge on the Newton Abbot by-pass, across the Teign at Hackney.

The Port Way passed along the ridge of Little Haldon, and utilised the spur at Ashcombe Tower, before it continued on a bee-line for Cofton Creek and Cockwood. Today for much of its length it is followed by metalled roads. In the past this Port Way formed parish boundaries on its northeast section. Larger scale maps bear out its existence and Port Road, near Shutterton, presumably led up to the Port Way.

At Castle Dyke (SX 922 770) an encampment was sited on a focal point of routes. The grid reference is given because Haldon has two Castle Dykes and there are also three Home Farms to add confusion to location details!

The coming of the motor car prompted greater improvements in the main roads. Kennford proudly had a by-pass opened in 1931 by the Minister of Transport, Mr Herbert Morrison.

In post-War times traffic increased drastically, with South Devon becoming a prime destination for holiday-makers. The Exeter By-pass, in pre-M5 days, became congested with traffic and was filmed every Bank Holiday showing streams of vehicles forking off at the Haldon Thatch. Laybys at the top of Haldon were often seen to be full of overheated cars whilst ingenious vendors patrolled the endless queues of cars selling newspapers, ice creams and other items.

The building of a new route over Haldon Hill and on to Plymouth has passed the jams on to the Tamar Bridge on the peak weekends of high summer. The ultimate solution might be a dual carriageway all the way to Land's End where the cars and caravans would disappear over the cliff top like lemmings!

The routes over Haldon can now accommodate several thousand vehicles per hour at such peak times with great efficiency. However there are those who are lulled into not realising just how fast these roads can be. A good case in point involved film actor Hugh Grant, who achieved international recognition for his starring role in the film *Four Weddings and A Funeral*. In April 1995 he was clocked at 98 mph, as he hurtled homewards down Haldon Hill, at Splatford near Kennford. He had been filming Jane Austen's *Sense and Sensibility* in Cornwall and following the week's shoot was in a hurry to get home...

Within 24 hours of Hugh Grant being clocked over the speed limit, globe-trotting walker Ffyona Campbell, of Totnes, suffered the same fate through the lens of the same speed camera.

Undoubtedly it is the speed exhibited by motorists crossing Haldon, on the main routes, which results in such a small proportion of them turning off onto any of the byways to discover the delights of these wooded hills. My theory is that the people who enjoy exploring the Haldon Hills are mainly residents from the South and East Devon areas. Holidaymakers gravitate towards Dartmoor, because everybody has heard of it, when leaving their coastal holiday homes.

Fill Her Up!

Logic is a wonderful thing and although it's not such a potent force as it used to be, it still has an important part to play in shaping how things turn out. Imagine the

Haldon Thatch filling station as it looked in its early days

well-oiled cog-wheels of the mind turning over in the man who first saw the need for a cafe and filling station at the top of the steep gradient of Telegraph Hill. He would have seen how the earliest automobiles would have struggled to attain the summit, then he would have gazed around him to see that the land wasn't prime agricultural land, also unsuitable for most development, so perhaps would be available at a modest price. And so it was that Haldon Chalet Garage was established, beside the Haldon Chalet Cafe (original telephone number Kennford 24), the combination being an early version of the motorway services. The garage proprietor also had the advantage of the extra trade generated by the way Telegraph Hill caused so many cars to overheat whilst heading towards the tourist towns of Tor Bay. Roadside repairs and recoveries made for a healthy business.

The buildings of those establishments are shown here as they appeared in their glory days before the age of mass motoring. The garage is no longer a filling station but is still there, several feet higher than the present A380. The Haldon Chalet Cafe is now a private residence. However, there is a most popular transport cafe on the same site. Behind is a chalet park which attracts many summer visitors. The view, which is on private land, is one of the best in Devon.

In adverts placed in guide books, during the 1930s, it claimed that it was sited in 'The Most Beautiful Spot in Devon'. Ray Cattell passed this way in the early 1930s and wrote this in his book, *Adventure Through Red Devon*: "Next morning we drank coffee in the keen air outside the [Haldon] Chalet on the Exeter road and watched the silvery morning mists pouring slowly like a glacier down the broad valley of the Exe. I doubt if there is any more delightful scene in Devon, for the connoisseur of views, than that from the top of Haldon." Of course there were less trees in the way in 1934!

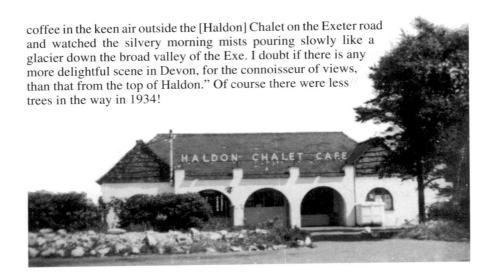

Bad Weather

Whenever bad weather is anticipated in Devon it is the Haldon Hills which seem to attract the worst of it. We know that Dartmoor is statistically worse and that places like Princetown get completely cut off at times when blizzards hold sway, turning the moors into a desert of white. However, Haldon attracts just as much publicity from the media's meteorological reports. Local newspapers delight in sending their photographers to the top of Haldon or Telegraph Hill to capture the wintry scenes of cars abandoned by the wayside. Gritting lorries make it their number one priority, as we have here the unusual coincidence of two important routeways, that is the A38 and the A380, rising independently, almost side by side, over a steep hill range. Global warming hasn't, apparently, done much for these hills!

Statistically Haldon is not all that extreme, with an average annual rainfall figure of just over 1000 mm per annum, and snow days far less than the upland moors of Dartmoor and Exmoor. However, motorists passing over Haldon regularly will often notice that the summit is crowned in low mist with adverse conditions prevailing. How often is the weather completely different on the other side of this escarpment?

In the past some unusual meteorological phenomena have been witnessed here. Glazed frost, which is rarely experienced in Britain, lasted for several days at the end of February/beginning of March 1929; hereabouts it is known as 'the ammil'. The press were obviously impressed by the phenomenon as many reports were made about it. Glazed frost occurs when certain conditions prevail to create supercooled rain. This precipitation is several degrees below normal freezing point but falls in a liquid state. This condition is so unstable that as soon as the supercooled rain touches anything it freezes instantly. On Haldon it was observed that bushes, fences and trees were all coated in this unusually clear transparent ice, nature's equivalent of lamination. Long grass, which had received several coatings of glazed frost, became so solid that it had a petrified appearance. Many branches and small trees could not support the dense, extra weight of the glazed frost and fell unceremoniously to the ground. Considering the vast amount of vegetation on Haldon, the damage done to almost every bush and tree must have been considerable. In some spots the glazed frost attained a thickness of half an inch.

Raymond Cattell summarised Haldon weather in his book *Adventure Through Red Devon* as follows: "When a too passionate summer drugs the senses in the rich valleys of Devon a man may regain his soul by climbing to the keen, bracing air, the sparse vegetation and the clear remote views of Haldon; but in winter its foreignness has a less attractive face, and when the lowlands are benevolently mild I have seen arctic views on this scarp and felt a bitter frigidity which does not belong to Devon."

Devon County Council have also felt Haldon's frigidity. In 1980 they embarked on an experiment which would ultimately save them thousands of pounds. At the top of Haldon Hill they set in the road an ice detection unit which is linked to Broadwalk House in Exeter (via Kennford) and to the motorway maintenance unit at Sowton. This highly sophisticated piece of equipment provides such data as wind speed, air temperature and, most important, road temperature. Over a given period the Haldon ice detection unit proved that several pre-saltings were unnecessary. This saves a lot of money when you consider that in present prices it costs a 'small fortune' each night to pre-salt many sites. They are expensive installations but their reliability has saved far more in the long term than their initial cost. Today there are more than thirty such devices monitoring road temperatures around the county.

From a conservation viewpoint these units are not conspicuous. Devon County Council have taken measures to ensure that they blend in with existing road surfaces in both texture and colour. The one on Haldon Hill is on the south bound carriageway near the apex of the hill beside the Exeter Racecourse.

The exposed top of the escarpment can often be as much as 8°C colder than the sheltered combes in its lee yet despite this, the conditions within the forests are often sheltered, and they experience their own micro-climate.

Key: A. Telegraph Hill   B. Haldon Hill   C. Former A38   D. Haldon Thatch   E. Woodlands
F. Smokey Joe's spot   G. Haldon Racecourse   H. Round O Plantation

Observing such stark conditions makes it seem even more of a mystery why the hills should have become home for so many Gentlemen of the Road, in the past.

GYPSIES, TRAMPS AND THIEVES

The Haldon Hills are inhabited by a number of folk and, as far as researching this book went, none were more helpful or obliging than the late John James, a well-known gypsy.

In order to discover details of events occurring in the Ideford area I was directed to his gypsy encampment at the top of Willwright Lane, below the lovely gorse-covered moors of Ideford Common. He had been recommended to me by John Pierce, landlord of the Royal Oak at Ideford, as a person who would be able to provide information about the area. His local knowledge, and willingness to impart it, was remarkable.

It was a sunny morning in October 1981 when we stood above his encampment on Ideford Common, leaning on a rustic fence, to talk about his family's adventures and stories of the area. No reference book or endless literary research could match the narrative content that John James expounded that fine day, all those years ago, as we looked across the countryside.

He began by identifying all the hills, valleys and settlements that you could see from this wonderful south-facing slope. He was a little perturbed that many other folk had also seen the loveliness of the view and made him offers for his little kingdom.

His family originally came from Cornwall, long ago, to this spot, which was originally on a stage coaching route. This was of a strategic importance as, with most gypsy families, they had a great knowledge of working with horses which provided them with plenty of work in this area. Indeed, the love of horses had been passed through many of the family's generations. John James' 'Grandfather Penfold' made a healthy business out of buying shell-shocked army horses after the First World War. With care and attention he worked wonders with them.

John James, likewise, loved these animals and devoted much of his time to buying and breeding them. He kept about twenty horses and used some of them to pull carriages. He had various pony traps that he used for weddings, charity work and ceremonies which required one horse power rather than several hundred. Most of his appointments, for hire, were within the Exeter and Torbay area. His care of his animals and traps extended to maintaining them personally and expertly. He shoed his horses and tended to most of their ailments, having learnt some pretty unusual cures from his grandparents. He even kept many chickens to provide eggs for a particular remedy that he favoured in maintaining healthy animals. Typical of his cures was the one for 'worming'. He administered a dose made up from a teaspoonful of turpentine and a pint of linseed oil. His lifelong ambition, which he was not to achieve, involved horses. Given enough money he would have happily emigrated to Australia or Canada to set up a stud farm.

But our conversation was not totally about animals and cures as John James produced several anecdotes about the area where he lived, only some of which are included here.

A Terrifying Sight

In about 1924 his grandad sat in the sun smoking his pipe in this idyllic setting with views to Dartmoor, beyond Milber towards Torbay and right across the South Hams. Suddenly this bliss was manifestly interrupted as around the bend in Willright Lane came a sight which really terrified him. It was the first motor bus in this country and, not having seen such a monster before, he was truly afraid. The single decker, which had set out from the Western Garage at Newton Abbot, was on a pioneer run. On board were about twenty passengers, several dressed formally in bowlers. After the initial astonishment a little realisation set in as this form of transport was going to be a threat to his business. Within years the same bus replaced the horse and trap, operating between Bovey Tracey and Haytor, for visitors ascending to Dartmoor. His greatest fears had reached fruition.

The James family demonstrated a knowledge of how to use the environment skilfully to provide a living. John James' grandfather earned two shillings and sixpence (12^1/$_2$p) a day by going into the woods, in the Ideford area, to collect ferns, which were bundled and then sent to Covent Garden. These were preferred to paper in setting off the various items on sale. He managed to collect about ten dozen bundles a week. Likewise John James occasionally supplied trees to local shops at Christmas time.

Hairy Willey

There is a large house at Thorn's Cross, 'Waddon Brakes', which had, at the time of this interview, just been given a new lease of life. I had often wondered why and how such an imposing dwelling had fallen into such a decayed state. John James explained its fascinating life story.

About 1920 a local giant of a man, called Willey, and his wife occupied the dwelling. Owing to his densely-bearded growth he was known to all as 'Hairy Willey' and this colourful character earned his living by collecting firewood to sell locally. He used a pony and trap regularly for his shopping outings to Chudleigh two miles from his house. To supplement his income he painted pictures on two-hundredweight corn sacks. When he died in 1928 the house lay empty and tramps used it as a passing through 'guest house' and as, gradually, the floorboards were utilised as heating fuel, the place fell into decay. A temporary respite occurred around 1960 when the house was purchased. It was renovated considerably but only lived in occasionally. Resentful wayfarers showed their contempt by regularly breaking the windows and effecting other structural damage. Some locals still refer to it as 'Hairy Willey's place'.

As we chatted, John James paused only briefly between stories. He gave me as much help as he could, proving conclusively that the best way to learn about the environment is to talk with families who have lived in an area for many years.

John James was a most colourful contributor to the original Haldon Hills book. Sadly he died in September 1990 at the age of just 57, after suffering a massive heart attack. Many hundreds of people attended his traditional Romany funeral at Wolborough Church, Newton Abbot. A red-wheeled horse-drawn carriage, lent for the day by a friend, carried his coffin to the church. It was pulled by 'Handsome', a black Welsh cob, one of John's twenty horses that had won first prize at a show in Kingsteignton just days earlier. A measure of his local fame and public standing was the front page coverage of his funeral in the Newton Abbot edition of the *Herald Express*.

'Smokey Joe'

The man has gone but his memory lingers on. I wonder how many regular pilgrims to the South West and Torbay in particular will remember an old tramp who lived on Telegraph Hill, Haldon. He was known as 'Smokey Joe' to the local population and won the hearts of many passers-by for no obvious reason.

In the early 1970s he drew the attention of the media and subsequently his fame spread, making him a living landmark on the Haldon Hills.

Smokey Joe derived his name from the colour of his face. He would make a fire

regardless of the temperature and sometimes in hot weather the exercise would seem to be merely routine. His success rate in fire lighting was questionable as there seemed to be an awful lot of smoke and very little flame. Thus his face was embellished with a blackness that was so distinctive. One of the regular police patrolmen visiting Telegraph Hill referred to his appearance as resembling a 'smoked haddock'.

Smokey Joe spent a great deal of his life at Doublebois Quarry near Dobwalls in Cornwall. There he was a familiar sight, pushing his pram along, as is often the case of vagabonds whose worldly possessions travel in tandem with their owners. Doublebois Quarry was disused at the time and Smokey Joe sought out a small cave perilously located close to the main A30 road.

In addition to the inherent dangers of the location of the cave, the hazard was made more acute by Smokey's presence. His smouldering embers would waft across the road posing an obvious threat to those unsuspecting travellers unaware of his unusual existence. The problem was further compounded by those who did know him and accordingly slowed up to gape or throw presents to him. Often a local fruit company's lorries discharged their remaining cargo. The near-accident rate soared somewhat to make the appropriate authorities consider the wisdom of allowing Smokey to remain.

Inevitably the cave was sealed and Smokey moved up the road for a while. His appearances, often with two ladies of the road and their respective prams, became less frequent. He moved on to Fraddon in Cornwall for a while before 'emigrating' to Devon. The word 'emigrate' is used advisedly as the Cornish think of themselves as a separate nation.

It is not known how Smokey made the journey into Devon. He may have been a stowaway on the Torpoint Ferry or even taken the route over the Tamar Bridge along with the queuing masses. His most likely exodus route was via the Cornish border village of Gunnislake, which has been for many years the home of several vagabonds.

The last two years of his life on Haldon saw many jet-propelled sandwiches and other goodies fly his way. On one occasion when he went missing local school children organised a search party for him. They were greatly relieved to see him return to his familiar spot after a week's holiday. If he had gone back to his original Cornish site he may have been saddened to see that his former residence had disappeared through a road widening scheme (without a hint of compensation).

Bus loads of returning commuters to the Torbay area would wave fervently even after a hard day's work in nearby Exeter. Such was the charisma of Smokey Joe.

Not a great deal is known of the man other than that those who stopped to speak with him were unanimous that he was a quiet person with a gentle humour. It is known that he often said how much he loved to share his wooded hillside with the birds, squirrels and stags that he looked on as friends.

In the summer of 1975 passers-by observed that all was not well. Within twenty-four hours the local police force had received more than twenty calls from worried motorists. The police officers found it difficult to persuade Smokey to go to hospital for treatment, or even an examination. However, another concerned passer-by managed to reason with him and he reluctantly went to the Royal Devon and Exeter Hospital. Smokey had a serious liver complaint, which resulted in a prolonged hospital stay. The media gave him both regional and national coverage from which the response was phenomenal; enquiries about his progress came from far afield.

The various organisations that dealt with Smokey had great difficulty in making arrangements as they could not discover his real name. Consequently, it was impossible to contact relatives. On admission to hospital Smokey Joe had claimed he was called Goldsmith whereas other people had mentioned the name Allsop. The consensus of opinion suggested that he was really Wilf Morgan.

He recovered sufficiently to leave hospital but as a long convalescent period was needed he could not return to his now empty spot on the Haldon Hills

Mrs Nora Andrews had befriended Smokey Joe in his earlier Haldon days and thus welcomed him into her 'Sydney House' guest house in Alphington Street, which was also often frequented by other 'waifs and strays'. This 'tramps' hotel' has since been demolished or 'trampled' and a new block of flats stands on the site.

Smokey Joe settled in well and it seemed that he was on the road to recovery. At Christmas 1975 he had a set-back and returned to the Royal Devon and Exeter Hospital for further treatment. It was discovered that his condition had further deteriorated. Shortly afterwards in January 1976 Smokey died at the hospital in Exeter. Again there was plenty of public concern and sympathy. Mrs Andrews had grown fond of the gentle tramp and was upset at his death so laid a floral tribute at his spot on Telegraph Hill. It was envisaged that a permanent memorial should be erected in his honour.

Many would argue that it is wrong to honour a person who opts out of a more conventional life style contributing little to society. Smokey Joe probably paid an expensive price for his freedom. Even the relative luxury of an overcoat and duffle coat worn through most seasons was not enough to carry him beyond his fifties.

The pictures on the front cover of both the original book and this one were taken on the same occasion in the mid 1970s by a former colleague, and fine photographer, Mike Williams of the Exeter Camera Club.

Harcombe 'Flats'

Smokey Joe was just one of many who were attracted to the Haldon Hills. Here are examples of some of the others who chose starry skies and damp hedges in preference to four walls and a roof.

Life certainly creates many interesting thoughts and analogies. At Torquay, guest houses and 'Bed and Breakfast' establishments compete for a still declining market. As a result they set high standards of accommodation providing such comforts as colour TV, bathroom en suite, heated swimming pool and so the impressive list of trappings available continues. Sadly many of the facilities offered will not be utilised, as 'vacancy' signs flutter in the breeze more in hope than expectation.

Nearer to Exeter, beside the A38 at Harcombe Bends, is a damp dark and disused limekiln. If it had borne a similar sign, some years ago, it would have said 'No Vacancies'. The limekiln saw continuous habitation for at least twenty years. Many who passed by, often at breakneck speeds, failed to notice this residence adjacent to a dangerous bend. Others who passed at a more leisurely speed often mistook the limekiln for a cave and probably failed to appreciate its once strategic importance in the world of vagabonds and travellers.

A cave it certainly is not. Above it, about a hundred yards distant, is the disused Harcombe Limestone Quarry now passed by the other half of the split A38 dual carriageway descending from Haldon. The quarry is barely discernible as since its closure many bushes and trees have helped to blend it into the environment. The limekiln has also become decked in creepers and other forms of vegetation thus making it harder to see when driving past.

Its habitation began, on a full-time basis, in the early 1960s when a host of estranged visitors took up residence, much to the annoyance of certain local authorities and to the disgust of some members of the public. In 1963 it was decided not to evict the residents but to allow them to persevere in their Bohemian-style existence. The 'cave dwellers' must have seen the limekiln as a residential limbo. Its cavern-like darkness was natural enough with its singular lack of facilities, but it provided shelter from the worst vagaries that Haldon weather could offer.

The limekiln attracted very many vagabonds but, from amongst the many residents, the only one whose name I could discover was a female tramp known as Mrs Ryder. But it did transpire from researches and interviews conducted that the limekilns were known as 'The Flats'.

As 'The Flats' became fashionable and populated an unofficial 'Central Bureau of

Tramp Movements' in South West England evolved. Legend has it that if a Gentleman of the Road needed to be contacted a message delivered to 'The Flats' would be dispersed to every lay-by and doss house in the peninsula within hours!

During the 1970s and '80s a lone, dishevelled person made the Harcombe limekiln his home. In nearby Chudleigh he became such a familiar sight that the locals fondly bestowed him with the unofficial title of 'Earl of Harcombe', but usually referred to him as 'Vic'. His frequent journeys between his home and Chudleigh were made by a bicycle that, thanks to the attention of a local garage mechanic, remained semi-roadworthy. When he first appeared on it the wheels had a distinctly squarish appearance which made his journeys even more perilous.

I tried to interview him on a few occasions yet somewhere there was a gulf between us which sadly resulted in a more superficial portrayal than such an interesting character merited.

Maybe upon reflection and in retrospect the 'Earl of Harcombe' deserved his bit of privacy. I suspect that he possessed the alcoholic entitlement of a lime burner without the discomfort of the heat normally associated with working limekilns.

Alas he, too, has passed away and one of the few pictures that I managed to take was this one as he walked across the road at Chudleigh's church.

Lofty and Ginger

Two other gentlemen, who will be remembered 'around and about the Haldon Hills', are 'Lofty' and 'Ginger' who spent many years there before their passing. Above 'Woodlands', in a small tributary valley of the River Kenn, a sizeable group of tramps gathered some thirty years ago. Their numbers reached about a dozen at the peak of the tramp population on Haldon in the early 1960s but dwindled gradually through the 1970s. Lofty and Ginger remained there until more recent times and became well known and to some extent well respected by the local community.

Lofty suffered badly from the vagaries of Haldon weather. When he got frostbite in his leg it resulted in hospitalisation and, sadly, amputation. Lofty left his home in these woods, which he had always called 'The Castles' and went to stay with Mrs Andrews, the same lady who had tried to nurse Smokey Joe. When he died he left Ginger as the main resident.

Ginger's real name was Arthur Pinnegar and unlike many of his contemporaries he enjoyed a much longer life. He left his North Devon home at the tender age of eight years and moved into the Haldon area. He spent a lot of time on the 'Trehill' estate near Kenn. In the village he was known and liked because his disposition was of the giving type. He often bestowed the children of Kenn and Kennford with sweets. He drew a social security pension after a life in which he worked when he could. In later years he helped out locally, cutting grass and hedge trimming in an unpaid capacity.

His existence continued in a typically rough and hard setting. His home was an extremely small hut of Heath Robinson design standards which was so low that only the lying down position was appropriate. It was supported by piles of magazines,

Around & About The Haldon Hills–Revisited

wooden struts and a tarpaulin canopy which completed the materials. Within it Ginger carried on through all the seasons. By night he would use candle after candle, getting through literally thousands in his

time there. By day he favoured a triangular shaped field lower down the valley closer to 'Woodlands'. Here he made a fire and sat by it for hours. His milk and bread were delivered to him by the respective roundsmen who called on him regularly.

Ginger must have been fond of cats as quite a feline population gathered around him. His only apparent dislikes were bathing and cutting his finger nails. Needless to say they grew to a bizarre length. He was active and very healthy until well into his seventies. Sadly a harsh winter took its toll, and he began to deteriorate.

After a short illness he died at Dawlish Cottage Hospital. A friend described it as a happy release as another winter would have seen him endure much suffering.

In their heyday Ginger and Lofty made a formidable duo. On Saturday nights they visited the Teignmouth Inn in Exeter. This cider house was sited near St Anne's Brewery, close to the mediaeval Exe Bridge. After a night of revelry they would catch the last bus back to Kennford. If Ginger made encouraging advances to young ladies returning home, Lofty would put him quickly in his place with his massive hand upon Ginger's shoulder. Ginger would usually submit.

The duo often visited Kennford. Lofty always bought one of the more intellectual daily papers and read almost every item with interest and understanding. Villagers still speak highly of Lofty and his appetite for hard grafting work. With Ginger he

would gather pramfuls of moss which they transported in their own inimitable way to florists and undertakers in Exeter.

Ginger is buried in the cemetery at Kenn churchyard. His grave is marked with a small wooden cross made by one of the villagers. When I visited his grave it seemed such an apt spot for his final resting place. It is at a high point in the cemetery, with views towards his former Haldon home. On his cross is simply written

'Ginger'. On a commemorative flower container were some withered flowers, inscribed on the bowl is his full name 'Arthur Francis Pinnegar' and the dates 1905-1980.

All the villagers of Kenn and Kennford will certainly remember him as will many of the passing army of motorists.

In the years that have elapsed since the first edition of this book I have been called on a number of times to give talks based on the book. Although it's true that everyone remembers Smokey Joe, the reaction to any mention of Ginger and Lofty, in the area where they were known, is nothing short of amazing. In the eyes of the many who knew them they were held in great affection and I have only ever heard high praise about them.

The Open Prison

Close to the former site enjoyed by Ginger and Lofty was an Open Prison, which is now closed!

In compiling a book of this nature it is necessary to write many letters making requests and asking favours from strangers, local experts and various authorities. One of the more helpful agencies was Exeter Prison who complied with my every request. I am grateful that the book was written when it was for now the site is devoid of almost everything that once stood there, save the clock tower and that is without its radiant little clockface. Here then is what I learnt and saw of an institution that only lives on in people's memories and photos like the ones in this book.

This prison, which was set facing the Exe Valley on the east facing scarp of Great Haldon, certainly did not resemble the traditional sort of institution, with towering high walls, conjured up in most people's minds. The restraining walls were substituted with hedges at Haldon yet even these were not intended for purposes of remand. The ideology of the prison was geared to rehabilitate men and prevent them becoming recidivists. The theme was 'service to others' and we shall examine later how this was made practicable. First it is necessary to examine the camp's origins.

Before the Second World War the many-hutted camp was used a Ministry of Labour Instruction Centre. Men from depressed areas came to Haldon to learn new skills in order to give them hope of employment in new spheres.

A waiting list of thousands hoped to be selected for one of the twelve-week courses on offer. The camp opened in November 1936 and accommodated one hundred students. It was hoped to double this figure.

The men had to be between the ages of eighteen and forty-five years, preferably single. The range of occupations offered included forestry work, road making, carpentry, metalwork and boot repairing.

After a 7.15 a.m. breakfast the men worked a four-hour shift before lunch, another afterwards. On Saturdays the work ended at midday. When free from evening lectures the students were permitted to leave camp as long as they were back by 10.15 p.m.

In 1949, Haldon Camp's life as a prison began, which was to span twenty-five years before its closure in 1974. A visiting dignitary in 1950 was impressed by the camp's statistics, which claimed that at least ninety percent of the intake would never return for further institutionalisation.

The camp was set up to cater for short-term prisoners. The courts did not send offenders directly to Haldon; as Exeter Prison had jurisdiction over Haldon it was up to them who was sent there. The type of offence committed, and the personality of the prisoner involved, were carefully considered before he was placed at Haldon. Inevitably the freedom and lack of physical constraints prompted some prisoners to ask for the more conventional high-walled surroundings, as they felt they could not trust themselves in an open prison set-up. The number of absconders was few as most

of Haldon's guests were serving sentences of less than one year. The only reason a prisoner might flee without permission was in the event of domestic problems — for example, infidelity.

For many it is easy to appreciate that their stay on Haldon would be perhaps one of the best things to happen to them. In almost idyllic surroundings, the outdoor life and a stable routine could be for some the first time they had ever had the opportunity to reflect on their own situation.

The buildings of the camp were huts, seven of which were dormitories, whilst others included a chapel, a theatre, a games room and an enormous canteen. There were also administrative buildings and, of course, the workshops.

The former football pitch resembled the side of Snowdon, and has since reverted to farmland. Mountaineering boots would have surely been more suitable on this pitch than football boots! This once staged matches, sometimes refereed by Ron Crabb, a famous former Football League official. He was also, as a warder, in charge of prison industry at Haldon.

Many stories are told of prisoners sneaking out into the nearby forest to meet girlfriends or collect hidden parcels. One ingenious lad from South Wales would

disconnect a Forestry Commission Land Rover speedometer and drive it around before returning it later. This cunning caper lasted a month before the mystery, of why a full tank of petrol could disappear without the vehicle having apparently been anywhere, was solved.

A free-standing clock tower, believed to be one of only twelve in Devon, stood at the centre of the Camp and enabled routines to be scheduled accurately. It was built in 1957 by George Musto, a brick layer working at the Camp.

The prison industries, with the trade mark 'Prindus', had enterprises such as a metal-stripping contract. A more agrarian activity was growing blackcurrants, which were sent to Holloway Prison to be made into jam.

A one-time, unpopular assistant governor appeared in a play at the camp theatre, put on for a mixture of prisoners and invited guests.

Towards the end of the production he recited the lines, "I must away, I must away." Appropriate in such circumstances, yet when he tried to exit from the stage he found that the backstage crew had barred his way by nailing the door closed. This created immense hilarity.

The warders who worked at Haldon Camp were sorry to see it close as it was a more relaxed regime in which to work. Staffing it was easy as many wanted to work there.

But now the prison is just a memory, the prisoners and the officers now having moved on to pastures new and the site overgrown at the time of writing. About the only thing that survives is Mr Musto's clock-tower, minus its clock. What a tale it could tell.

LORDS, LADIES AND GENTLEMEN

In the Georgian era both sides of the Haldon Hills saw impressive mansions and estates develop as wealthy merchants, traders and entrepreneurs used their newly acquired fortunes to create splendid homes.

Within this chapter is an attempt to describe only some of these estates and the various notable families who graced the Haldon Hills. Although not specifically noted, there was much social interaction among the wealthy elite.

Through economic circumstances and a changing social climate these estates no longer possess such powerful and wealthy dignitaries. Some of the great houses are still lived in, whilst others have become flats, offices, hotels or schools. Few continue in the manner, or the manor, to which they were once accustomed.

Elizabeth Chudleigh

One of the late keepers of Lawrence Castle, Mr Dale suggested that no book about the Haldon Hills would be complete without mentioning the story of the infamous Elizabeth Chudleigh, whose family had a long Haldon history. A lot of time was spent on their estate called 'Place Barton' at Ashton. Her story is an unusual one which deserves fuller exploration.

Elizabeth Chudleigh was born in 1720 at Harford, a small village in the Erme Valley on Southern Dartmoor. Her early years in such remote surroundings were to be in stark contrast to her later life. The probable reason for the following events is attributed to her incredibly beautiful looks.

William Pulteney, Earl of Bath, was on a shooting party in the vicinity of Harford. He was so taken by her beauty that he overlooked her lack of finesse and education to obtain for her a position as Maid of Honour to Augusta, Princess of Wales, which realised her a vast salary. However, shortly afterwards she married Augustus John Hervey, a naval lieutenant. The wedding took place at 11 p.m. on 4 August 1744 at Winchester and later was to provoke much controversy. Not wishing to forfeit her income as Maid of Honour, she kept the marriage a secret. Although the match was not successful, a son was born.

George II was reputed to be fond of Elizabeth and organised a masquerade in her honour. He also gave her a very expensive watch, and her mother was appointed Housekeeper at Windsor. Elizabeth caused quite a stir when, in the masquerading character of Iphigenia, she appeared almost nude at Somerset House. The Princess of Wales was not amused!

In 1750 she moved to Knightsbridge and took up residence with Evelyn Pierrepoint, the second Duke of Kingston. This was a longer relationship, allowing Elizabeth the chance to enjoy the fruits of immense wealth, which records show she did with great style.

Unfortunately for Elizabeth events played a cruel twist. Her real husband, Augustus John Hervey, sought a divorce, and she in turn tried to show that her first wedding was only a pretence by instituting a suit of Jactitation of Marriage, which resulted in the Annual Register of 1769 freeing her from any contract with Hervey. She was then eligible to marry the Duke of Kingston and the marriage took place in

March 1769, lasting four years until the Duke died. Fortunately she was to be well provided for, as she inherited a vast fortune. The former Duke's nephew, who had missed out on the inheritance, set about trying to prove that Elizabeth's first marriage was still valid, in an attempt to inherit the fortune himself. To complicate matters, Hervey became 'Earl of Bristol' following his brother's death. If the first marriage was upheld, Elizabeth would become 'Countess of Bristol'.

At Westminster Hall in April 1776 hundreds of people queued for tickets to witness the bigamy trial, which caught the imagination and curiosity of the public. It lasted six days and resulted in a 'guilty' verdict. Elizabeth claimed Benefit of Peerage, which absolved her from an undignified prison sentence.

She left England and travelled to several countries. Czarina Catherine made her welcome in Russia where she bought a mansion near St Petersburg, which she called 'Chudleigh'. Her plans to 'Anglify' the grounds were never realised as she died in Paris in August 1788. Her last spoken words were: "I will lie down on the couch. I can sleep and after that I shall be entirely recovered." Wrong!

Her will requested that her body should be laid to rest in Chudleigh, Devon. A large sum of money had been set aside for a monument to be erected at Chudleigh Church but her wishes were never fulfilled. Surely, here is a story that playwrights could exploit as its twists and turns almost beg to be dramatised.

The Other Chudleighs

Beneath Ashton Church is an old farm called 'Yarde'. It is sited beside 'Place Barton' which was originally the manor house of Ashton. Like many landowners, Sir Hervois de Helion received a parcel of land from William the Conqueror. The Chudleighs later possessed this Manor from 1320-1745 and experienced many colourful and sometimes tragic events in their time at Place Barton.

Sir George Chudleigh was created a Baronet in 1622 and exhibited a fine sense of equilibrium by fathering nine sons and nine daughters. In the Civil War he started out with the Parliamentary forces but, after the undignified defeat at the Battle of Stratton on the Devon/Cornwall border, he changed his allegiance to the Royalist cause. Sadly his son James was killed at Dartmouth.

The family title ceased on 1st August 1745 when Sir John Chudleigh was killed at Ostend when he came second in a duel! The house was left to fall into ruins. It is possible that some of the materials used in building Lawrence Castle (1788) were from the remains of Place Barton. A lake which existed to the north of the house was filled in, and a deer park above it has also gone. A public right of way exists from the site of Place Barton up this small valley towards Doddiscombsleigh passing a mixed wood called 'The Forestry'. It is possible to see some of the remains of Place Barton but appreciating its lovely setting provides greater reward.

The Manor of Ashton is now sited in Lower Ashton having changed hands. Near Spara Bridge (1604) over the Teign in Lower Ashton is the Manor Inn. This is a small unpretentious inn with plenty of atmosphere, not too much ceremony and a lovely warm open fire!

Lawrence Castle

When you have tortuously climbed its ninety-nine steps you may feel that you are on top of the world, but consultation with the Ordnance Survey map reveals that you are only about 900 feet above sea level. However, when you step through the door 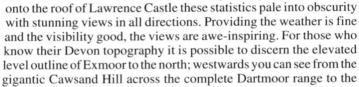 onto the roof of Lawrence Castle these statistics pale into obscurity with stunning views in all directions. Providing the weather is fine and the visibility good, the views are awe-inspiring. For those who know their Devon topography it is possible to discern the elevated level outline of Exmoor to the north; westwards you can see from the gigantic Cawsand Hill across the complete Dartmoor range to the  rocky outcrop of Brent Hill; south eastwards from the duned hills of Dawlish Warren the eye reaches Sidmouth Gap and beyond; and to the north east the Blackdown Hills become prominent with the Wellington Monument visible through binoculars. On the brightest of days even the Quantocks of Somerset can be spied.

Lawrence Castle is better known locally as Haldon Belvedere, and was built as a memorial to General Stringer Lawrence who founded the British Empire in India. The story is long and interesting, these being some of its more important details. The word 'Belvedere' means a small pavilion or turret on top of a building, open to the air on one or more sides. The word is Italian in origin meaning 'fine view'. In that context it is apt but while there are many 'belvederes' in Devon, there is only one Lawrence Castle.

For many years Lawrence Castle was occupied by two brothers who loved their building, despite the primitive conditions in which they lived. They refused to give in to commercialisation but with little cash to spare could only allow the tower to deteriorate. Nevertheless they had an immense knowledge of the history of their 'castle' and their great affection shone through when they talked about it.

On a quiet, hot summer afternoon, in 1981, I sat down with the Dale brothers to find myself spellbound by their anecdotes, wisdom and humour. Here are just some of the facts behind the story of Lawrence Castle, one that begins with an almost rags to riches story.

Robert Palk was born at Ipplepen near Newton Abbot in 1717 and was from a poor background. He went to India in the 1740s and was befriended by Major-General Stringer Lawrence. This contact saw Robert rise to the position of Governor of

Lawrence Castle before vegetation grew around it.

Madras, an extremely prestigious and important title. At the same time he traded in many ways, using his position to influence and benefit Indian princes, other traders, and himself. He creamed off the best deals and amassed a great fortune.

The Haldon Estates were owned by the Chudleighs prior to this but their family died out. Now Sir Robert Palk, he acquired this estate of about 11,000 acres which stretched from the edge of Haldon across the Teign Valley towards Dunsford.

A bachelor, Stringer Lawrence often left his London home for extended stays with the Palk family. His favourite spot for exercising his cocker spaniel was around the site of Lawrence Castle. Major-General Stringer Lawrence died in 1775 at the age of 78 and is buried at Dunchideock Church. After he died Palk had the Castle built as a memorial to him and it was completed in 1788. The Palks also perpetuated the name Lawrence in the Christian names of their sons in following generations.

The building was used occasionally as a summer house but more so as a place of entertainment, when frequent use was made of its small ballroom.

The original floor was imported from the East Indies by Sir Robert Palk. Many people took the trouble to write or tell me that they often attended wonderful tea-dances that were held at the tower.

Down the family line the Palks acquired the title Baron. The first Baron Haldon (Lawrence Vaughan Palk) was a developer who owned almost three-quarters of the land in Torquay and St Marychurch. Sir Robert Palk had bought these lands from Arthur, Earl of Donegal, in about 1768. This Baron Haldon built Haldon Pier and Hesketh Crescent, plus many fine Italianate style houses and buildings in the fashionable and fast-growing Victorian resort. Hesketh Crescent is named after Lawrence's wife, Mary Hesketh.

At this time Lawrence's son, Lawrence Hesketh Palk, dabbled in gambling and within eight years of inheriting the title became bankrupt. The estate was sold off and broken up.

The tower changed hands a number of times. Mrs Dale, mother of the two Dales who spent so many years at the 'castle', bought the tower in 1933 for the princely sum

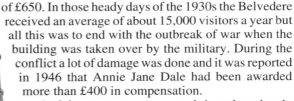

of £650. In those heady days of the 1930s the Belvedere received an average of about 15,000 visitors a year but all this was to end with the outbreak of war when the building was taken over by the military. During the conflict a lot of damage was done and it was reported in 1946 that Annie Jane Dale had been awarded more than £400 in compensation.

And time moves on apace and since those heady days when this book was first written the Dale Brothers have both died. At that time I was unaware of the third brother, now also deceased, who had fallen out with the family and, although he only lived down the road at Ide, had not spoken to his brothers for over fifty years.

The best way to learn more about this famous landmark is to go out and visit it now

The tower before restoration, with one of the Dale Brothers just visible to the right

that it is fully restored and renovated. The work cost just under half a million pounds but the contractors did a marvellous job, however, don't just take my word for it – go and see for yourself!

Haldon House (The Lord Haldon Hotel)

It is Haldon House where the Palks lived out such a splendid existence. Only the east wing still remains of the original Haldon House, which was once enormous. In January 1982 it became 'The Lord Haldon Hotel'.

The date of its construction is debatable as a variety of possible years are suggested, the earliest being 1717 and the latest 1735.

Sir George Chudleigh, whose family had long resided at Place Barton, Ashton, had Haldon House built. When he died in 1738 the estate devolved to his three daughters and co-heiresses. On a division this became the property of Sir John Chichester who married one of the daughters.

Sir Robert Palk bought the massive estate with his Indian-made fortune. His income was further increased when Major-General Stringer Lawrence, a bachelor, died leaving him another £50,000 – a colossal amount by Georgian standards (and mine!)

Apart from its size Haldon House possessed art treasures, which included paintings by Weenix, Snyders, Claude and Rembrandt. A picture of Stringer Lawrence, painted by Sir Joshua Reynolds, also adorned the walls. To enhance the setting of the house, 200 acres of plantation were begun in 1772.

Through time Haldon House saw many great people come and go. George IV was a frequent visitor and, in order that he could attend balls at the Lawrence Castle Ballroom, a special drive was laid between the house and tower. The route is still visible today with the specially constructed bridge near to the entrance of The Lord Haldon Hotel still intact. The route meant he did not have to travel the same road as commoners like us!

Another famous and frequent visitor was Marconi who was a friend of Gerald Bannatyne, a son of the family who bought Haldon House when the estate split up. Marconi did several experiments in the area, often using Pen Hill, the site of Lawrence Castle.

In Dunchideock's church

The Palks' connection with Haldon House was severed through Hesketh Palk's gambling addiction. Hesketh's son married a famous Russian dancer and they produced the last Palk, Lawrence Edward Broomfield Palk. Despite his impressive name he died penniless at Westminster Hospital in 1941 aged 46. His sole income was fourteen shillings and elevenpence (75p) per week from National Health insurances. From rags to riches to rags!

Haldon House had deteriorated from its original grandeur and in 1925 it was advertised for sale: "The Mansion built by Sir George Chudleigh in 1717 is a fine example of Georgian architecture. The reception rooms are large with heavy mahogany doors. Billiard Room. Theatre and about thirty bedrooms. The private chapel is detached from the mansion with stained glass windows. Good seating for one hundred. Electric light. Central heating. Modern drainage. Pleasant grounds and

park about thirty-six acres. Late owner spent £100,000 on mansion. This will be sold for demolition about the middle of September unless previously sold. Price £8,500."

It was not until the 1940s that the main demolition work took place. The east wing is all that remains, this now being the present Lord Haldon Hotel. It has been a hotel for more than thirty years having had several owners. The Preece family are working extremely hard to make use of the wonderful site. The Lord Haldon Hotel lives on in the shadow of so much history.

Oxton House

You might be tempted to skip this section as the name and house will probably be unfamiliar to you. You may also consider an old country house, particularly one you don't know, is as exciting as a potted aspidistra. But Oxton has a past full of incident despite its secluded location. No major roads pass near to this fine old estate. It is tucked cosily into the south eastern side of Great Haldon and enjoys a very sheltered site in a small wooded combe, about two miles west of Kenton, a village which has played a great part in Oxton's past. It has its own private road and therefore enjoys great seclusion and peace.

Adam de Oxton built the first house nearby for his new bride and chose the highest navigable point on a tributary of the river Kenn for his 600-acre estate.

Alexander de Oxton was later given the right to journey through the farmhouse at Ashe on condition that he was en route to Mass at Kenton. Apart from these few obscure details a great void appears in the old records. The old house disappeared and its story is vague until Nicholas Hurst appeared in Elizabethan times. He left Oxton to his sister who had married William Martin, who had various talents as an author and historian but made a fortune as a lawyer. He died aged 55 years with his younger widow soon marrying one of the Courtenays of Powderham. The line of Martins struggled on to 1770 when William Clifford Martin died childless and left the estate to Nicholas Tripe of Ashburton.

Young Nicholas was fortunate in respect of inheriting not one but two estates at the same time from different benefactors. He changed his surname from Tripe to Swete and opted to live at Oxton. He erected the present house in 1781 having the picturesque gardens and lake landscaped.

In the middle of the nineteenth century the Studds arrived in the form of William Mortlock Studd. He was so enamoured of the place that he wrote into his Will that when he died his body was to be interred in Oxton soil. His dying wish was fulfilled on 6 December 1877 when Oxton soil filled his grave in the quiet north-east corner of Kenton churchyard. His eldest son then took over the estate and lived up to the family name by producing six sons and six daughters, in quick succession, early in this century.

Life at the house is well documented and in 1897 an impressive list of workers was employed there. Within the house was a butler, footman, two housemen, cook and scullery maid. In the extensive grounds were six men and a boy in the gardens with two carriage boys in the stables. Outside of the gardens were a headkeeper, two woodmen, painter, wheelwright and six farmers. Each week it is reputed that a sheep was killed from the resident flock for consumption.

Ernest Studd, a younger brother, managed the estate but had sufficient time to be Master of the Haldon Terriers.

Life for the resident workers was hard, as one would expect during that era. The working day in 1897 was from 7 a.m. to 6 p.m. except on Sundays. Lubbock's three Bank Holidays dating from 1871 provided some occasional respite but work was the order of the day.

Those who lived in were expected to go to church on Sundays, dressed in their

Sunday best. The workers walked two miles along the lanes in all weathers to Kenton church whilst Mr and Mrs Studd travelled there by horse and coach. This was stabled in the yard of the 'Devon Arms' now on a dangerous bend of the A379 in Kenton. The Master enjoyed enforcing the Victorian demand for punctuality at services and woe betide anyone who was late!

The Studds showed more lighthearted qualities when a few pageants were held in the grounds. In 1909 an Ivanhoe Pageant was staged and another entitled 'The Betrothed' followed in its wake.

After 1918 Studd sold the house to an Irish Peer and moved to a walled estate just to the north of Starcross.

The Earl of Listowel bought the house in Devon, having suffered when the marauding 'Sinn Fein' movement had burnt down his mansion in Ireland. Perhaps the original 'Irish Joke' was made complete when some of his own men sought revenge and burnt down the main pub in nearby Bally Hooley. Alas, this too was the property of the Earl of Listowel!

He settled in well to the more peaceful air of Oxton. He relaxed to the extent of pottering around the estate in such a shoddy state of dress that visitors frequently mistook him for a gardener. Despite great wealth, this would seem to be a common trait amongst the wealthy.

Within the grounds of Oxton, close to the East Lodge, is an unusual but listed feature, a Hermit's cave. This cave is cut into the red sandstone rock in an intriguing fashion. Unlike grottoes, which tend to be damp, dark and generally dingy, this cave is warm and dry. It must have provided good shelter for its one-time lone occupant. Carved from the wall of rock is a shelf which provided a seat of natural stone and above this is a cross carved into the rock. The cave, which has a regular rectangular shape, is also situated in one of Devon's most sheltered vales, providing extra insurance against our oft-times inclement weather. Some people speculate that this was not a genuine Hermit's cave but more of a Victorian folly.

Oxton was a girls' school with a roll of about fifty young ladies aged from eleven years upwards. Their main contact with the outside world was on Sundays when they were transported by bus to Kenn church. The parade of immaculate uniformed young ladies would have surely rivalled the most elegant 'Come Dancing' formation team in both appearance and co-ordinated movement into the pews.

Alas, economies and other problems finally closed the school. Miss P. W. Donkin, Headmistress, accepted the closure philosophically as the school merged with Shute School at Axminster. Shute shared the same type of curriculum and entered the same examinations. Only a few pupils and teachers were left misplaced.

In 1966 this 'much sought after' property came onto the market. The advert placed in the newspaper went something like this: "This imposing residence, particularly suitable for school, institution, convalescent homes or for conversion into flats (subject to planning permission). Sold with vacant possession. Price £26,500."

It was converted mainly into flats after the subsequent planning permission had been granted. Again a 'Martin' appeared as owner, this time being of 'Martin's Caravans' fame.

The tranquillity of Oxton was shattered several years ago when some young men found themselves on the roof of Oxton. They chanced across one and a half tons of lead which they took as a memento of their visit. They were arrested for their souvenir hunting. Despite their protestations of innocence, they were convicted.

With Kenton church, like many others, in need of repair, Oxton staged a fashion show in 1971. It was a success and the well known local vicar, the Rev John Parkinson, gave due thanks to both spiritual and practical overseers.

The lake at Oxton, which measures 850 feet by 150 feet, was purchased by a Mr Wallace in 1963 who set up a wildlife sanctuary there. Most notably a flock of Canada Geese became regular visitors.

Mamhead House (Dawlish College) and Park

Was it the yew tree or his life-long friend that made the famous diarist and biographer James Boswell vow never to become drunk again? Certainly it is sure that this solemn vow of abstinence from alcohol was made under the yew tree, believed by some dendochronologists to be about three thousand years old, at Mamhead church (St Thomas), on the south eastern end of the Haldon escarpment. The vow, which was to be broken often, was made in the presence of the Rector, William Johnson Temple, who was teetotal, as were all the ensuing generations of Temples. This trait continued right down to his great-grandson, Archbishop William Temple. The enormous yew tree is not only on a list of registered yew trees but also believed to be at a holy site where some form of worship has gone on since at least the time of Jesus or before. This species of tree has long been favoured for graveyards. Perhaps its eternal sombreness, or maybe its poison leaves, shoots and bark, prompted the well-known remark that even horses despise yew trees!

James Boswell, a Scot, had befriended Temple whilst they were both students at

Edinburgh University. Boswell became famous for writing the biography of Samuel Johnson. Temple was his second great subject and influence. He could not have been too happy on his visit to Devon, as Temple had described the accommodation at this rectory as in a 'wretched condition'.

Temple was an interesting character and at times an unlucky one. His own father had become bankrupt and, to improve his own plight, married into money only to discover that his father-in-law had also become bankrupt. To improve things he applied for a 'living' abroad but as his talents were great, and appreciated, he was given a 'living' in Cornwall worth six times more than at Mamhead.

Although Mamhead and its park form a quiet corner of the county, it has nevertheless experienced some notable events and buildings. Its name means a hill shaped like that of a teat. This was probably the last thing on the mind of Lady Gascoigne Nightingale who was struck by lightning whilst walking in Mamhead Park. Sadly she died in her husband's arms and was laid to rest in Westminster Abbey. Her spirit is said to haunt the grounds occasionally, but does she travel to Devon from London, for this haunting, via the M4/M5 or the A303/A30?

Many local people will associate Mamhead with the fine obelisk that can be clearly recognised from many locations in the Exeter and Exe Estuary area. There is a well defined track to it from a nearby car park on Haldon. Disappointingly, it bears no inscription, but vandals have etched their names onto it. One notable carving is 'Enfield Meth YC 62' which is deplorable.

Research reveals little detail about the obelisk. It seems it was erected between 1742 and 1745 by Thomas Balle. The hundred-foot high pillar is made of Portland Stone and was created as a navigational aid to shipping in the English Channel. The views from the base of the pillar are magnificent and many fine woodland strolls can be enjoyed in its vicinity. In 1994 a specially laid out trail for wheelchair users was opened by Lady Tebbit.

The quality of the scenery has attracted many wealthy gentry who in turn have employed the best architects. When the Earl of Lisburne acquired Mamhead House in the eighteenth century he employed Robert Adam, one of the greatest architects of all time to refurbish it. He built the Orangery which remains as a residence to this day, whereas the original house was demolished in 1829. The Orangery was built with Bath stone and possesses a gazebo (a turret or lookout point) providing more than a modest-sized home. Records show that orange trees were grown there in 1833 being placed out of doors in square wooden containers during the summer months.

Mamhead House was rebuilt in 1828, its architect was Anthony Salvin. It was Mamhead which made him his name and launched him on a career which saw him become the top architect for Tudor-style country houses. Capability Brown landscaped the grounds to complete the classic nature of Mamhead. The importance and status of the 350-acre estate could be seen in its own red-brick church, which is not a Victorian whim or fancy but an earlier building dating as far back as 1250. Although one of the smallest churches in England, it still sees some service lying within the parish of Kenton.

Mamhead House has seen many notable events. From a powerful telescope Sir Peter Balle was the first to discover that Saturn had more than one ring. In the second half of the nineteenth century Sir Lydston Newman satisfied his overwhelming passion for horse racing by owning several racehorses. The top floor of the house is still referred to as the 'Jockeys' Rooms'. Sadly Lydston amassed enormous debts and, following his death in 1892, many of the possessions which passed to Sir Robert Newman (who became Lord Mamhead) had to be sold off including the Ashcombe Estate.

During the Second World War Mamhead House housed many historic treasures and records in its extensive cellars. This included the Bishop's Throne from Exeter Cathedral, which was reputed to be the finest wood carving in Europe. A bomb fell on Exeter Cathedral at the exact spot where it had been sited. In 1949 when it was returned after restoration and repair, the event was deemed so important that the Queen (then Princess Elizabeth) attended the ceremony to mark its return.

Within Mamhead Park are some strikingly beautiful trees that have drawn 'arborealists' from great distances to observe them.

Thomas Balle in 1686 was the first person in England to raise trees from acorns. He introduced Cork Oak, Wainscott Oak, Spanish chestnut, Acacia and Cedars of Lebanon. Seeds taken from the world's tallest tree, a giant redwood, which was growing at Bull Creek Flats in North California, were planted in 1943 by Lord Mamhead a few years before his death. A Turkey Oak with many of its lower branches 80 feet long is thought to be the largest individual tree in Europe and its canopy shades an area of almost one acre.

Mamhead House holds some personal memories for me. When it was a private school, known as Dawlish College, I attended an interview for a job there as a teacher of Geography and general subjects. A few years later, in 1982, I was invited by teacher Harry Wooltorton, to go back there. This time it was to play soccer against the 'boys', a lively set of lads from a variety of backgrounds, mostly bad, the school having had a change of direction with the type of pupil that went there in the late '70s and early '80s. This led to the 'Mamhead Matches' between my former 'Over 35s' keep fit class and the boys becoming regular, fortnightly, games played on long summer evenings in the mid 1980s. The only concession to age was the fact that instead of having two halves there was only one half and we played downhill for it! But all good things come to an end and the school eventually closed and the place was bought by a development company.

Dawlish College in the days when it was a private school

Mamhead is in a backwater of narrow, twisty and steep lanes but the countryside is well worth exploring. Brian Carter's book *Pub Walks in and around The Haldon Hills* will tell you just how worthwhile!

Ashcombe Tower

Ashcombe Tower is no longer the type to conjure up the image of a damsel in distress waving a handkerchief whilst a gallant knight seeks to extricate her from captivity. However, as the picture of the tower from the past shows it could have been that sort of place. It was built in 1833 as an observatory and later a shooting box.

It was originally owned by the Holman family of Holcombe, who let it deteriorate. In the 1930s, when the parents of the five Holman children died, little enthusiasm was shown to keep the tower in the family. Only Hester, one of the Holman's daughters, made a significant bid to keep the tower. She even made a token attempt at converting the tower into a dwelling.

Brigadier Sir Ralph (then Major) Rayner, MP for the Totnes Division, bought the tower and almost two thousand acres of land in the surrounding countryside. Hester was crestfallen by the sale. Soon afterwards, whilst horse riding nearby on Little Haldon, her horse reared and she died from the fall. She had exhibited a rare talent as a sculptress and had produced many fine black and white lithographs of subjects from the Ashcombe area. One of her brothers was married to the film actress Vivien Leigh.

The Rayners employed architect Brian O'Rorke to design them a house. Within the plan they encompassed the tower which had become dilapidated so it was necessary to gut it and it became the main staircase in the new dwelling. The oak flooring came from the British Museum, which was being renovated.

The 1934 residence had a garage large enough to accommodate four cars and its own petrol pumps.

O'Rorke managed to adapt the wonderful hill-top site to create a house with a sunny aspect. Servants' quarters were created on the upper floor and two bachelor guest rooms were designed on the lines of a ship's cabin.

Ashcombe Tower houses a unique souvenir that Sir Ralph Rayner collected at the end of the Second World War. He was amongst the first troops to enter Berlin and also the first to enter

Hitler's bunker 'The Eagle's Nest'. Amidst the obvious confusion he saw one of Hitler's personal telephones and pulled its wires from the wall. He then smuggled this trophy back to Ashcombe Tower. He tried to connect it up to our telephone system but found it to be impossible. This remains as possibly the most fascinating relic to be found in the Haldon Hills.

Since these details were first published there was a story printed in the *Daily Telegraph* of another Westcountry man, called John McCowen who also claimed to have Hitler's personal telephone. He was a British Intelligence officer who made two unauthorised visits into the bunker. His other collected artefacts included the 'pull' from Eva Braun's lavatory and an authenticated diary belonging to Heinz Linge, Hitler's valet. Perhaps then there were at least two telephones or someone might have got their lines crossed...

Sir Ralph was always an active man, and his efforts for Haldon Racecourse are noted elsewhere. He organised a twice-weekly bus service from Ashcombe to Dawlish and set up an annual one-day, Pony Club event which attracted a top class field. Sir Ralph lived an extremely active and successful life. He was Tory MP for Totnes from 1935-1955 and was knighted in 1956, two years later becoming High Sheriff of Devon before he died in 1977.

His widow, the late Lady Rayner, was the daughter of Samuel Courtauld. In her time there she entertained many famous visitors to Ashcombe Tower. Neville Chamberlain, en route to Slapton Sands, stayed overnight after landing on the nearby Haldon Aerodrome.

Lady Rayner was amused to learn that 'CB' radio enthusiasts had given Ashcombe the code name 'Fawlty Towers'. When we photographed Hitler's telephone it was impossible to resist the temptation of an imaginary conversation between Basil Fawlty and the former dictator. "Don't mention the War," seemed appropriate.

In the land where the unusual seems to be the norm, a final bizarre connection exists between the late Sir Ralph Rayner and the landlord of The Royal Oak at Ideford, John Pierce – each of them once owned Totem Poles. Sir Ralph shared John Pierce's enthusiasm for these unusual landmarks which stood so proud in the Devon landscape. Sir Ralph was President of the Devon County Show Committee on three occasions and, to mark his last term of office, he presented the totem pole which has appeared at so many County Shows.

THE UNUSUAL

This is an umbrella title for a series of strange, even bizarre and outrageous happenings, occurring around and about the Haldon Hills. As befits my fascination for the curious and 'the unusual' this is a strange blend of mystery, history, religion, crime, violence, conflict and genius. To get in the right mood we'll start with a few pubs.

The Highwayman's Haunt

There cannot be many people who enter pubs or inns with the express intention of learning something of interest either about the locality or about some historic events. It is nevertheless true that, by examining the walls and even other parts of inns, it is possible to learn a great deal. This is certainly so at the Highwayman's Haunt on the old A38 just on the outskirts of Chudleigh.

As its name suggests, it has taken advantage of a possibly true saga about a certain highwayman called Jack Withrington who was reputed to have used the chimney breast of this building when hard pressed by pursuers. The house was then called Row Hill (meaning Rough Hill) but is referred to in various old accounts as 'Rowells'. Rowell Moor is close by just north of the A38.

Withrington was one of five sons who all died by the hangman's noose. He was a local folk hero who helped himself illegally to other people's possessions on the Exeter to Plymouth highway. He paid highly for his not-so-dandy deeds when he was hanged at Tyburn on 1 April 1691.

Around the walls of this luxurious pub is a collection of paintings, sketches, commentaries and so on of 'Gentlemen of the High Toby' from all over England.

Like other pubs in the Haldon Hills there is an educational excuse to visit it. Parts of the building date back beyond Edward I's time and it has been proved that a Saxon settlement existed on the same site. It was a restaurant for many years and became a pub in 1968.

The Nobody Inn

People like to joke about visiting this well known inn, "What's the point of going there if there's nobody in?" Perhaps, in a time warp sort of way, they are correct. One of three stories pertaining to the name of the Inn strongly suggests that visitors to it, at one time in its long past, may well have found no landlord or lady to serve them. The couple were so fond of going to market they would forsake the Inn trusting people to serve themselves. Hence as the first people arrived, they found nobody in.

Finding it these days is not really difficult, as it is so well signposted that the maze of narrow lanes to it are easily followed. Possibly though many will lose themselves on the way home again as the signs are not reversed to allow a similarly easy return to civilisation! Several years ago the Nobody Inn cashed in on their location by challenging people to find them. People liking such adventures took up the challenge. By seeing how busy the pub gets at certain times it seems that either the publicity exercise worked well, or that Devonians are very gifted map readers.

At some time in the early 1500s the Inn came into existence when it was converted from a cottage. It was not embellished by the same home comforts, high quality cuisine or fifty-plus whiskies that it boasts as part of the present-day Inn. For its first few hundred years it served the local farming community mainly as a 'cider house'. It must be stressed that the type of cider sold then was a much more heady brew than is served these days.

The Inn has limited accommodation, invariably being full, reflecting the high standard on offer. To wake up to a breakfast served in the bedroom on a fine morning in such lovely surroundings must be a delight.

Two other possibilities of the origin of the name arise. One of the past landlords who died was so fond of the Inn that he never wanted to leave it. At his funeral in nearby Doddiscombsleigh it was generally thought that when his coffin was interred at St Michael's it bore no body. This, I am assured, is the correct version or so the late Bill Rowland of Ide insisted.

The last of the trilogy concerns another landlord of the Inn who was about forty years old. He was wealthy and ran the Inn very much at his whim or fancy. If he did not like the look of potential customers he did not answer the door and pretended that there was 'nobody in'.

An attractively designed sign on the outside wall seems to suggest this story as possibly the one with the most credibility, but who knows?

St Nectan's Church, Ashcombe

In the upper reaches of the deep combe of Dawlish Water is the beautiful St Nectan's Church at Ashcombe. Possibly it is to the Haldons what Widecombe is to Dartmoor. Although it does not possess a legendary group like Tom Cobley and company to immortalise it, it does have a legend which is unusual.

Nectan was supposedly the eldest child of the Welsh Prince Breccanus. His twenty-three brothers and sisters (remember it is a legend) probably made life so unbearable that he set sail from Wales to land in North Devon. Compensating for his earlier life style he set himself up in a hermit's cell near Hartland in that area.

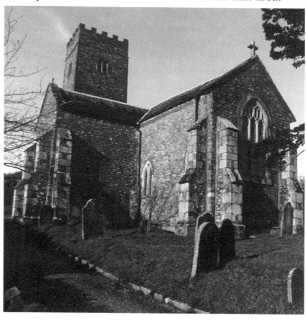

One morning Nectan awoke to find that some robbers had stolen his cows. Protecting his interests, he sought to find them and eventually discovered the robbers. Being religiously inclined he preached at the robbers but to no avail. They acted militantly and cut off his head. This did not please Nectan but he picked up his head, tucked it under his arm, and strolled back to his lair. Where his blood dripped foxgloves are said to have grown.

His brothers and sisters followed him into the area and one of them became St Morwenna who gives her name to Morwenstow in North Devon. 'Stow' means religious, holy place or shrine.

Nectan's canonisation may be attributed to the number of miracles wrought at his tomb. Three churches in Devon are named after this Welsh saint; the other two are at Hartland and Welcombe, both in North Devon.

The Roselalehem Trust — Clarice Toyne

Clarice Toyne was a natural mystic. Throughout her life she had a series of visions which led her through meditation to extend her awareness. She lectured on subjects like reincarnation, which she believed in wholeheartedly. She sought to set up a centre which would be utilised to expand her work to involve people from all religions, all walks of life and from all corners of the world.

Consequently her family moved into 'Lakeham' just beneath Lawrence Castle. The site was ideal for her work with peace and the unquestionable beauty of the Haldon Hills and its vistas. She visualised a Lay Monastery, hoped to be the first of many. At first a marquee was used for a summer festival. Dr Westall, then Bishop of Crediton, presided over and spoke at the first meeting. The second festival suffered from the vagaries of Haldon weather. The need was there for a more permanent and substantial building. Amazingly, after a short while, the money was forthcoming. The Roselalehem Trust, which was set up, began to work well with Tibetans and all manner of visitors attending conferences. The 'New Look' or 'Message of Inner Truth' spread.

Unfortunately Clarice Toyne was stopped in her tracks by the death of her husband. Their peace and tranquillity had been shattered by the news that a route for electricity transmission lines would pass their home and centre. Mr Toyne, a solicitor, took on the job of trying to prevent the line of pylons. He suffered a coronary thrombosis, and the Trust was closed down.

Mass Exodus?

At Easter, some years ago now, a massive orienteering event, involving several nations and around four thousand participants, was staged in the area usually set aside for more leisurely strolls. This was a team competition following in the wake of an individual event completed on Dartmoor a few days earlier.

The impressive spectacle went ahead with Forestry Commission officials appearing afterwards to see how much litter and debris remained. They were pleasantly surprised to find that absolutely nothing remained to indicate that four thousand or so people had ever been at the spot, apart, that is, from one sad little lead toy soldier standing resolutely on top of a post.

An Irish team, with some time left on their hands, knocked on the Chief Forester's office and asked permission to use one of the picnic tables. John Brain was then very surprised when they set up the table as an altar, donned the appropriate gear and celebrated Holy Communion in the woodland glade.

Lidwell Chapel

On the side of Little Haldon, near the golf course, are the remains of Lidwell Chapel. Many stories are told of a monk who would lure passing travellers into the chapel and, once there, he would rob and murder them, but not necessarily in that order. The corpses were then disposed of down the well.

Lidwell is believed to derive from Lady's Well or Our Lady's Well. It is close to the source of one of Dawlish Water's main tributaries.

The chapel had a long history, being mentioned in connection with some foul deeds as long ago as 1329. Bishop Grandisson dispatched one of his men to make enquiries about Robert Middlecote, a clerk

of Lidwell. As a result of these investigations a trial took place on 1 June 1329, the outcome of which is not known, but Middlecote was guilty of defaming the Bishop. The likely accusation made was that Middlecote was a 'son of perdition' or a 'satellite of Satan'.

Both controversial incidents culminate in a more sensational happening. In about 1980 a Bristol photographer took a picture of the chapel remains and was amazed when the print revealed a fully formed chapel instead of the remains. Alas, although I hoped to include this, it proved impossible to acquire it.

If you go down to the woods…

Most people respect and enjoy the loveliness of Haldon's forests for the scented air, the occasional terrific views and, hopefully after reading this book, the history of the area. However there are those individuals who have gazed on Haldon's woods for nefarious reasons and who have used the dense vegetation cover as a place for their dark deeds. Here is a story largely gleaned from newspaper reports at the time.

In the summer of 1989 Keith Rose requested stock maps of the forest that showed all the various routes and paths. It appeared that he was trying to identify an old carriage route. With several site visits he developed an intimate knowledge of this area. Later information showed that Rose had also given the impression that he was a serious potential purchaser of Higher Ashton farm. However this was all a front for a long-planned abduction. Rose's kidnap victim was chosen partly to settle an old score. He had worked for business tycoon Desmond Cracknell's food firm but when Rose left the company he had been given a poor reference which left him bearing a grudge. Coupled with his own financial difficulties, Rose contrived to acquire a substantial ransom from a man whom he despised in order to ease his money troubles.

Late at night Rose, dressed in military combat gear, broke into his former boss's son's Surrey home brandishing a sawn-off shotgun. He left Mrs Cracknell gagged and handcuffed whilst, with his shackled victim, he sped through the night down to Devon – he knew exactly where he was going and how he was going to hold his hostage. Victor Cracknell was held captive, tied to a tree, for some four days with a rope around his neck, his eyes taped, and a substance like Blu-tack stuffed into his ears. Rose had a crash helmet, some reports stated that it was a collar, for Cracknell to wear. Whatever the device it had a wire which was attached to a car battery. If Cracknell tried to get away a severe electrical shock would be administered. Whilst Victor Cracknell endured this ordeal Rose went about his business. He even bumped into two forestry workers but after a brief conversation with him they never suspected that there was anything untoward about his presence there, and would never have imagined the news headlines that would follow.

Whilst the kidnap victim's nightmare continued deep in the forest, Rose was actively engaged in getting his ransom. Desmond Cracknell drove to Devon and deposited £142,000 in banknotes that Rose duly collected. Mr Cracknell then drove swiftly back to his Sussex home to await the next development but instead of Rose calling it was his son who had managed to escape despite the shackles holding him. In a short time Rose was arrested. He was subsequently found guilty and sentenced to 15 years at the Old Bailey but that wasn't the end of it for him. In another trial, in 1991, Rose was also convicted for a murder, which had taken place many years earlier, of the wife of another wealthy businessman. Juliet Rowe was shot dead at

Budleigh Salterton and as she had no enemies it had been difficult to find a motive for her callous killing. The police believed that this had been a kidnap attempt that had gone horribly wrong and, although Rose has continuously protested his innocence, the evidence was sufficient to result in a guilty verdict. Had he not carried out the Haldon kidnapping he would, most probably, have evaded the Juliet Rowe murder charge forever. He made the news headlines again, in 1995, when he escaped from Parkhurst, with two fellow inmates but was eventually captured still on the Isle of Wight.

Daylight Robbery

When this book was first published in the early 1980s, the Forestry Commission had a small hut, at Buller's Hill, where they sold copies along with other bits and bobs. However the woodland shop was broken into and the only thing stolen was ten copies of the book!

A Pair of Drakes

Sir Francis Drake was born at Crowndale near Tavistock and had many attachments with Plymouth. Therefore it's not at all surprising that these two places should possess statues of the great Elizabethan seaman. One stands proudly on Plymouth Hoe gazing out to sea to make sure that we don't get invaded again. It was placed on the tercentenary of his circumnavigation of the world. The other stands at a road junction in his home town and watches the traffic pass by. Both are beautiful statues that depict the man in bronze making him some ten feet tall. This was necessary for the idea was to create an imposing figure. But why am I telling you all this? The reason is that there is a third giant statue of Sir Francis, equally tall but made out of hard plaster, on the Haldon Hills!

As this statue is on private land I will not give its precise location but it is not an ornamental statue in anybody's garden. It lies beside the prostrate corpse of another headless sculpture in dense undergrowth and it would be easy to walk by it, at close quarters, without seeing it. It was borrowed from Exeter's Royal Albert Museum, in the 1930s and stood by a tea hut but the statues were never returned or reclaimed. The tea hut has since been reduced to

rubble, and is scattered about in the woodland. They say that Drake had the true spirit of adventure – perhaps the same should be said of his statues!

An Orange Elephant

The motorists who eventually reach the top of Haldon either by the A38 or the A380 will be confronted with several eating places. It could be that some entrepreneurs

have applied psychology in the siting of so many restaurants and cafes on the crest of the escarpment.

Most of the people who have purchased this book will probably reside in Devon and only be on short excursions, so will probably not have visited any of these establishments. The impression I got from visiting them was that the majority of patrons who were there were breaking up tediously long journeys.

At one eating place an enormous orange elephant can be found. Imagine the shock strangers to the area must have when the mist is down and they see this orange pachyderm looming out from the grey beyond! The elephant, which is almost life-sized, is strongly moulded to provide fun and relief for youngsters stopping off with their parents for such a break. The idea is for children to climb up a stepped rear and then slide down the trunk. It was discovered that 'elephantus orangus' was born in Tooting, London. Not much information about it is available other than it arrived in Devon via a trunk road!

Dog Cemetery – Buller's Hill (SX 877 857)

If you climb Buller's Hill from the direction of Lawrence Castle you will find a small overgrown quarry on your left. Beyond this at the top of the rise is a car park, on your left. From the A38 follow the ridge road past Haldon Plain, Buller's Hill's forestry headquarters and the Bird of Prey car park. Shortly beyond, and on the right,

is this unusual place. The sign at the entrance states that this is Whitepath Clump car park. If you venture into the trees at the north end of the car park you will find, beneath the shade of the trees, a considerable graveyard. Names like Trina, Sally, Dino, Percy, Bimbo, Lassie and Flossie indicate that these are not the graves of suicide victims but of dogs so loved by their respective owners that they have earned a resting place on the Haldon Hills, on which they no doubt scampered about before going to that great dog pound in the sky. Some of the 'critters' buried here now are rabbits, pussies, guinea pigs and other animals so the canine monopoly has been broken.

In the course of writing this book I visited the cemetery many times in the hope of

discovering more about the site, as the more accepted forms of research proved fruitless. It's been suggested that the first doggie graves were dug here just after the Second World War, indeed, some of the earlier graves now appear to remain unvisited and some have either been vandalised or have suffered from the vagaries of the weather. A few of the more substantial crosses bear messages like 'Flossie, Treasured Friend Rest in Peace' and remain intact. Other relics reveal graves which have seen better times. I can only speculate that in such cases the owners had either died or moved away. There has been a tremendous increase in the area now covered by doggie graves. They have also become more elaborate and ornate, possibly at the expense of the strange disappearance of some of the earlier graves. The graves shown here are just a random selection to convey an impression of what the pet cemetery is like.

A Forestry Commission official told me that, to his knowledge, only one dog owner had ever asked permission to bury their pet there. He was also surprised at the precise choice of location because the surface is covered in a layer of flints to a depth of several feet and this is a notoriously tough material in which to dig holes.

A Haldon Duel

A dramatic episode occurred on 10 May 1833 involving a much respected Exeter doctor, Peter Hennis MD, and a distinguished Irishman, Sir J. W. Jeffcott, who frequently visited Dr Hennis socially.

A rumour was passed around that Hennis had made some ungentlemanly remarks about Jeffcott's fiancée to her parents. Jeffcott, despite his worldwide travels, heard

about this in London. He stopped at Exeter en route to Plymouth, bound for Sierra Leone. Hennis thought it would be a good opportunity to clear himself of any blame and visited Jeffcott at his hotel. Before he got there, though, he bumped into Jeffcott in the street. Unfortunately, Hennis made a poor job of reassuring Jeffcott of his innocence and phrased his apology in such an unfortunate and inappropriate way that Jeffcott flew into a rage. Jeffcott set about Hennis verbally calling him some extremely unpleasant things. When Hennis asked for a retraction Jeffcott said that he would make sure that if Hennis did not visit him at his hotel before 2 p.m. he would spread the news that Hennis was a coward.

This all resulted in a meeting on Haldon at a place near the race course. Hennis was attended by Captain Halstead, a close friend whereas Sir Jeffcott was aided by Charles Milford. Hennis insisted before the duel that he disapproved of such practices and would not fire a bullet in return.

The two involved in the duel made their preparations and stood back to back. They paced off in opposite directions, but on the word 'prepare' Jeffcott misunderstood the instruction and turned quickly to fire at Hennis. The shot entered at a delicate spot on the right hand side of the doctor causing much pain and bleeding. Jeffcott, realising his error, was overcome with remorse and rushed across to the doctor uttering profuse apologies. Hennis, being the true gentleman he was, despite his great pain and obvious discomfort, reinforced that he had at no time said anything untoward about Jeffcott. Magnanimously he absolved Jeffcott from all blame over the shooting incident and fully forgave him.

Jeffcott drove off to Plymouth in order to board his boat. The others assisted Hennis back to Exeter where he died from his wounds a week later after suffering great agony. He was taken from his High Street rooms and buried at St Sidwell's church. There is a white stone tablet in Exeter Cathedral that bears no mention of the duel but was presented by his friends as 'a testimony of his private virtues and active benevolence'.

The law decided to prosecute those involved in the illegal duel. Almost immediately Captain Halsted and Charles Milford were charged with murder whilst officers hurried to Plymouth to arrest Jeffcott. When they arrived at the docks they discovered that his ship had already sailed for Sierra Leone. It was ironic that Jeffcott went there to take up the post of 'The Chief Justice and Judge of the Vice Admiralty Court'.

Rumour has it that on a later voyage to Australia he was acquitted of the murder charge, like the two 'seconds', and later returned to live in England.

Dr Hennis, aged 31, had an impressive funeral. Both Hennis and Jeffcott were Irishmen and share the dubious honour of being involved in the last Devon duel, and that beside what has now become a dual carriageway!

Hello, Hello, Hello!

A few years ago a car stolen from Exeter headed towards Torbay. An observant policeman lurking in a lay-by noticed the registration and gave chase. As the car was full of men the policeman radioed ahead and this resulted in a road block successfully stopping the car on Telegraph Hill. A Mr Marshall was arrested by PC Marshall, Sergeant Marshall was on desk duty and accepted the charge, and yet another Mr Marshall was very glad to get his car back. None of them were related!

The 'Swan of the Exe'

Journeys aboard trains passing the Starcross area must have been more lively in the past. From various travelogues it seems that every passenger would move to the right hand side of the train at Powderham to press their noses against the window to view the fallow deer on that estate, and then hurry to the opposite window before getting to Starcross.

This frenzied manoeuvre was made to witness a most unusual spectacle *The Swan of the Exe* and her sister ship (or tender) *The Cygnet* which were moored for many years in Starcross Harbour.

Captain George Peacock made the plans and specifications of the gracefully constructed swan-form yacht. Far from being a crank, Peacock skilfully calculated all aspects taken from enlarged measurements of a live swan. The beautifully carved neck and head rose sixteen feet above the waterline giving it the necessary majestic appearance of a real swan. It had an overall length of eighteen feet, a draft of seven and a half feet and a breadth in the beam of a similar dimension. It had a capacity of five hundred cubic feet, weighed five tons and could accommodate fifteen to seventeen persons.

One contemporary report suggested that it was designed by a Mr Wren, built by a Mr Fish for Captain Peacock. On one occasion when it went adrift a Mr Fox rescued it. In truth it was built by Dixons of Exmouth in 1860 and no Mr Fish has ever been employed by them.

The craft even more resembled a swan when a-sail, as its wings were snow white sails. Beneath, two ingenious swan-like feet, worked by a manual fire-engine handle which required four persons, propelled the craft.

The *Swan of the Exe* was built as a luxury craft with its interior like a first-class railway carriage. Ladies could pamper themselves in a boudoir sited in the breast of the bird. The seating throughout was bound in green Morocco leather.

This 'steam gondola' and its cyclodial propeller shared many happy and exciting times in the Exe Estuary. Many times it broke loose from its moorings and on some occasions even plummeted to the bottom of the estuary. In time it became unseaworthy and was hoisted over the railway at Starcross into the garden of Regent House, home of the Peacock family

This happened about 1936 with further deterioration taking place through the years. Its head snapped off but a replacement was made by a local railway porter. However, it eventually got into such a poor state that it was destroyed. Its tender, the much smaller *Cygnet* can still be seen at the Exeter Maritime Museum. It would be unworthy to deal with these unusual craft without mentioning the amazing deeds of their owner: Captain George Peacock of Starcross (1805-1883).

Starcross's famous son did more in his 78 years than might seem feasible. It is ironic that in a village so 'Brunel' orientated, another genius should appear.

At the age of 13, George Peacock was taken away from Dawlish Grammar School. He had excelled in chemistry and science and also became a fluent linguist in French, Spanish and Latin.

In 1822 he invented the first workable screw-propeller which was inserted in his father's brig, *The Fanny*. In his spare time he studied surveying and draughtsmanship.

Aboard HMS *Salamander* in 1832 he utilised his knowledge of chemistry to install an aerating device which produced pure sparkling water. This was so successful that the Navy transferred him to two other ships where he was requested to do the same again. Amazingly it was fifty years before he received a 'thank you' letter from Sir Garnet Wolseley.

His achievements continued with a medal from the Royal Humane Society for saving life in Quebec. The King of Bavaria presented him with a gold snuff box for some track charts that he had prepared for him. He raised a ship from the St Lawrence River despite jeers from doubting spectators, which earned him an inscribed plate and fifty-two pounds from an insurance company. In many ways Captain Peacock was a pioneer salvage expert, in the mode of Red Adair, recovering ships that many felt were impossible to raise. Insurance companies and underwriters were always financially grateful, but often not for several years after each event.

Another gold snuff box was received from King Otho of Greece for surveying work made with a view to linking the Gulf of Aegina to the Gulf of Lepanto. The Corinth Canal eventually followed this route between 1891 and 1893.

Near Panama there is a headland called Peacock Point. George had worked in that area only to discover that earlier charts were incorrect. Feet and fathoms had been muddled, which would have had serious consequences. He proved the charts wrong and thus had his name immortalised in the place name.

In 1831 Peacock left the *Hyacinth* to survey a route for a proposed canal to link the Atlantic and Pacific Oceans. After he had enlisted the help of a Spanish-speaking Indian he spent a week planning a route for a waterway of twenty miles length going half way across the Isthmus of Panama. He fixed the poles, proved that previously recorded data were inaccurate and also brought back a plan for a proposed railway across the Isthmus.

Capt George Peacock's grave at Starcross

A timespan of about half a century elapsed before the Panama Canal was first attempted. At a meeting in Liverpool, Ferdinand de Lesseps publicly acclaimed the work and skills of Peacock. The French engineer started to engineer the Panama canal in 1881 but failed when he tried to do it without locks, the two seas at either end having different tides. However the route that was later adopted was that of Peacock's, and this was forged, locks and all, between 1904-1914.

In South America he set up several experiments to test the corrosive resistance of various coated metals. Not surprisingly he used the results, from Valparaiso and other harbours, to invent a highly successful paint or coating to preserve iron ships.

In Chile he discovered a coal field which yielded thirty thousand tons for the Pacific Steam Navigation Company. He engineered a railway there before going on to extract beds of virgin guano and nitrate deposits in lands belonging to Chile.

As a merchant he carried the first mails from a host of South American countries and, still in communications, he improved the design of railway buffers, then set about similar improvements on sea telegraph cables. In his spare time he invented a life saving jacket.

Eventually he returned to Southampton and started the company of 'Peacock and Buchan'. In 1850 he retired to Starcross where he conceived his idea for the *Swan of the Exe* and the *Cygnet*.

In his retirement he remained active with detailed accounts appearing in local papers of his attempts to save Dawlish Warren from total destruction. He died in Liverpool but was buried in Starcross.

Forgotten Railways

During the First World War a Prisoner-of-War camp was set up on Kenton Common beneath Mamhead. The Canadian Lumber Corps staffed the camp whilst German prisoners were 'working guests'. The camp was set up to work the woods for timber that was so urgently needed in the war effort.

To transport the timber down the valley to Starcross an inclined light railway was constructed. The shape of the land was ideal as it dipped gently towards Starcross, which suited the horse-drawn wagons. The route followed the Staplake Brook in its lower section with odd remnants of the line visible in a few locations. For entertainment the Canadian soldiers visited Kenton and Starcross for weekly dances. They were not charged admission as it was felt they contributed adequately by consuming enormous amounts of alcohol. This suited the local girls and several of them married Canadians.

Another railway venture was considered in the 1930s when plans were considered to make a more direct rail link between Exeter and Newton Abbot. The frequent closures of the coastal section due to cliff falls or storm waves prompted engineers to examine a route from Exminster to pass below Mamhead, and strike south westwards towards Newton Abbot. A perusal of the Ordnance Survey map makes one appreciate how difficult this task would have been, but the Second World War dealt this scheme its death blow.

A Fine Man of Music

Exonians will probably remember some time in their life going down to the music shop in Exeter's Fore Street, one with a window that was always stacked with a vast selection of musical instruments from the smallest to the largest and from the shrillest to the deepest-sounding. The man who ran this shop with such enthusiasm was Bill Greenhalgh, a man of great energy who, sadly, is no longer with us. He lies buried at St Michael's, Dunchideock

and his unusual grave stone reflects his love of music and musical instruments.

Murder Most Foul

This chapter approaches its end with a bizarre episode that might be best forgotten. One September the badly decomposed, decapitated body of a young woman was found on Haldon. It set a grim puzzle for the detectives charged with the task of discovering the truth behind the origin of this gruesome discovery.

They didn't have much to go on. Fragments of bullet showed that she had been shot. So the forensic experts set to work on her clothing. Their first breakthrough came when a distinctive motif was found on the woman's tee shirt. This then lead to the USA and what some might feel to be a minor discovery ultimately led to the arrest of millionaire Michael Telling. The victim was his American wife, Monika, whom he had killed at their home in Buckinghamshire.

Michael Telling did not automatically dispose of her corpse but kept it at home whilst he, initially, kissed and talked to it. He kept her corpse in the house for five months until he felt the need to dispose of it.

Telling had lived in Devon before and knew the area well. He decided that the woods, in the area known as the Round O Plantation, might conceal his grisly secret for a bit longer. He drove her body to the spot, removed her head with an axe and took it home and placed it in the boot of his car. But Michael Telling hadn't reckoned with the expertise of the forensic department and the dogged determination of the detectives on the case. He was soon caught and stood trial at Exeter Crown Court. He was found guilty of manslaughter on the grounds of diminished responsibility and sentenced to life imprisonment.

THE LEISURE AND PLEASURE HILLS

An extremely varied range of leisure activities are pursued in the Haldon Hills, which includes horse racing, horse riding, hang gliding, model aircraft flying, motor-cross, rallying, trout fishing, jogging, walking, picnicking, shooting, hunting, and wildlife observation. The forests are so extensive that they can accommodate many hundreds of people without the landscape seeming overcrowded.

To assess the extent of each of these pursuits is impracticable within such a small book. I have selected three which are popular and are of great significance to the Haldon Hills. The racecourse, along with Newmarket, is the oldest track in the country. The walking potential is superb, with magnificent panoramic views to be seen in lovely surroundings. And within the deeper parts of the various plantations are found a wide variety of habitats producing an equally great diversity in the flora and fauna. It is these aspects which lead most people into taking an interest in these hills.

Haldon's Racecourse

The two-mile oval Exeter Racecourse takes jockeys so far from the mass of spectators that it is impossible to know exactly what happens as they gallop their way round this beautiful hilltop course. I have heard it said that they tell each other jokes!

It is probably a 'safe bet' to assume that most of the punters at the Devon and Exeter races know little of the great history behind this course. Horse racing in some shape

An aerial view of the racecourse. The A38 loops from centre right at the top of Haldon Hill, before disappearing off the top left towards Chudleigh.

or form has occurred on Haldon since the first meeting way back on 11 July 1769. Even then meetings were run on an established basis with fixed weights and stakes in compliance with an Act of Parliament made in 1740.

Meetings continued through the eighteenth century on a regular basis. Meetings were all-men affairs. The landscape was then much more open, with none of the vast forest of conifers that clothe the escarpment today, and commoners grazed their cattle there.

The nineteenth century at Haldon's racecourse wrought many changes. In 1804 women were admitted at the reduced rate of two shillings and sixpence ($12^{1}/_{2}$p), a tidy sum of money then, with only thirty-two takers. Attracting large crowds was made difficult by the location of the course. Journeys up Haldon's steep scarp slope were frequently difficult and perilous. The method of transport spectators used to get to the course revealed a person's status. On arrival they were often subjected to the vagaries of Haldon's weather where extremes were common. Haldon's high rainfall, frequent mists and generally lower temperatures combined to make a day at the races uncomfortable at times. Documented evidence reinforces this with many complaints about the bitter conditions reported in September 1825.

Lady Rayner making a presentation at the Exeter Racecourse

The glittering prizes presented to the winners were usually donated by Exeter MPs or by local dignitaries. The pattern of two days' consecutive racing was established with six flat races in each meeting. As there were two possible circuits, an inner and outer, the races were varied to provide an interesting programme or card.

The Enclosures Act 1813, as interpreted by the Commissioners, awarded the stands and part of the course to the Lord of the Manor, Sir Lawrence Vaughan Palk. The remainder of the land went to Henry Ley of Trehill near Kenn. The two men are

Around & About The Haldon Hills–Revisited

linked inextricably in a novel way as the village pub in Kenn is the Ley Arms but was originally the Palk Arms.

Following each pair of race days a banquet was held the day after. This was called the 'ordinary' and took place at differing venues. The dictionary defines 'ordinary' in this context as a public meal at a fixed time and place. In 1831 it was celebrated at the London Inn in Exeter and is said to have lasted many hours, being followed by a ball at the Devon and Exeter Showrooms.

At the end of the century a revolutionary decision was made. A meeting in January 1898 ended with a vote to adopt National Hunt rules and in September 1898 the first steeplechases were witnessed. It was felt that improvements were necessary, with £1,000 being spent on a new stand. The course made aviation history by erecting a

No mystery – it's Agatha Christie!

temporary hangar for an Around Britain flight in the early part of this century. Later a parade ring in front of the stand was completed making Haldon the third course in the country to have this facility.

Brigadier Sir Ralph Rayner was always a good patron of the Devon and Exeter Races. In 1969 he donated a Gold Cup worth £1,500 (1969 prices) to the winner of what has become 'The Haldon Gold Cup Steeplechase'. Although the course has had several famous visitors there are none probably better known, on a world-wide scale, than Agatha Christie who enjoyed the occasional day at the races on Haldon whenever she could. In fact she presented the Mousetrap Cup for a race that was run at the August meeting. In the true tradition of the long-running, record-setting play I can't possibly tell you who won each race and you'll have to go and see it for yourself!

In April 1972 an application was made to run several motor racing events at Haldon. Although the scheme received outline approval from the RAC, various opponents to the application managed to use enough protesting muscle to quash the idea. The Reverend G. F. Rickard summed up the viewpoint of many environmentalists when he said, "It is environmental pollution of the worst kind."

Nevertheless, environmental pollution of the second worst kind did come to Haldon in the form of longtrack speedway racing. The track within the racecourse was a costly construction with three partners investing a total of about £15,000 in the hope of attracting large crowds. Billing the biggest names in the world enabled crowds of 13,000 plus to visit Haldon. Alas, the fickle whims of the public saw a dwindling support with crowds sinking to a low of little more than one thousand. A costly venture ended in early 1981 with a decision to terminate their lease.

The translation of the word 'Haldon' is not entirely straightforward. One interpretation is that it means Holy Hill. Could this possibly be because of all the prayers offered up whilst the races are in progress? At least high up on Haldon you can be sure that they are a bit nearer to the Heavens.

Walking in the Haldon Hills

If you are a walker you will probably fall into one of two categories. You may be the type who likes to follow signposted routes marked by orange dots, acorns or other appropriate indicators, or you may be the type who dislikes the obvious constraints,

limitations and lack of adventure often attributed to 'packaged walks', preferring to chance your luck in the hope of greater reward. This section of the book will hopefully aid both walking factions.

Haldon Hill walking would be made far more respectable if the area was promoted to the status of a National Park or even a mini National Park. However, it is not and, partly for that psychological reason, many keen ramblers have never set foot on it for a stroll of any significant length. Yet these hills are not without interest and though tamer than the nearby upland moors, have enough variety to justify exploration.

For geographical and geological reasons, the top of Haldon is almost totally devoid of settlement. The unsuitability of the soils for agricultural pursuits has resulted in an upland area not as inhibited by hedges and fences as similar altitudes within the Exmoor National Park. Admittedly it is a man-made landscape in many parts but the deep combes with precipitous sides combine to provide a topography of great landscape value.

A word of warning is necessary if you intend to stray into the woods on unmarked paths. The paths shown on 1:50 000 Ordnance Survey maps are usually not the only ones which exist! Care should be taken to examine undulations in the terrain. A compass can also be of valued assistance as dense woodlands can certainly disorientate ramblers.

It is not in the woods nor on Haldon's top that I suggest you begin your perambulations. How can you possibly appreciate the grandness of the hills if you lazily begin on the top of them? There are many good starting points at the foot of the range. Logically if you are on a circular route you will benefit from a lengthy descent when you will most appreciate it, you will also ascend when you are at your freshest.

The Ordnance Survey map fails satisfactorily to identify land which is private and thoroughfares which may not be followed. The best advice I can give you is to remain on tracks and lanes until the upland area is reached. It is only a few large estates, like Whiteway, which seem to deter access.

The lanes beneath the Haldon Hills are usually traffic free. Those to the west of the range give good views to southern Dartmoor or the west side of the Teign Valley and its hill villages. Those to the south are more pastoral, true Devonian up and down affairs. To the east the scenery to be sampled is the lower Exe Valley, the expanse of the Exe Estuary, Woodbury's many commons and the East Devon coastline. As

the watershed is climbed the vistas and panoramas increase accordingly.

Pub Walks in and around the Haldon Hills by Brian Carter is a splendid little book containing seven walks in the area and gives a real insight into what these hills, and the surrounding countryside are all about.

Forest Trails

Describing potential routes is a dull task but attempting to lure new walkers into the Haldon Hills is the aim. In foul weather the sheltered nature of the woodlands may well appeal to those who have got to walk but feel that the upland moors would seem too extreme. The packaged walker is catered for during the summer months by the Forestry Commission who have trails of varying lengths which can be tailored to suit the

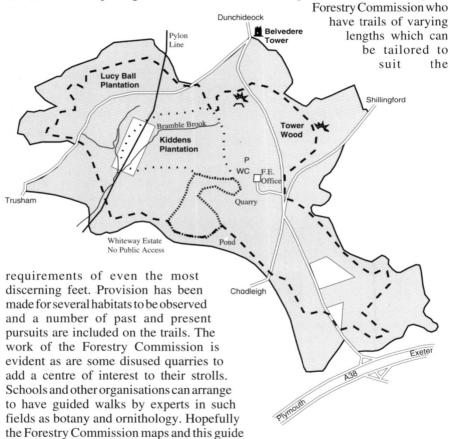

requirements of even the most discerning feet. Provision has been made for several habitats to be observed and a number of past and present pursuits are included on the trails. The work of the Forestry Commission is evident as are some disused quarries to add a centre of interest to their strolls. Schools and other organisations can arrange to have guided walks by experts in such fields as botany and ornithology. Hopefully the Forestry Commission maps and this guide will answer most of your questions. The great potential of walks possible on the Haldon Hills has only been partially considered. There is little open moorland left owing to afforestation following the Enclosures Act of 1813. Nevertheless the network of tracks and quiet lanes combine to make this an area to explore in a pedestrian fashion. The Forestry Commission trails are carefully staked out. Owing to problems of possible erosion on these soft tracks and to allow the Forestry

Commission to carry out their thinning and management programme, the trails are restricted to the summer months only. They more than adequately cover the northern part of Exeter Forest, with the longer trails taking in some breathtakingly beautiful scenery. Route details can be acquired from either the Forestry Commission Hut or from their nearby Buller's Hill Headquarters. For those who wish to do their own shorter strolls in

Baroness Tebbit opening the extension to the wheelchair path at the Mamhead Obelisk car park in August 1993

other parts of the Haldon Hills the choice of walks is immense. In the areas of Mamhead and Ashcombe are some beautiful strolls. For peace and beauty there are few areas of Devon better suited to walking than the Haldon Hills.

Another innovation at Mamhead, to tie in with the All Abilities Trail, is a small, native broadleaf woodland, known as Tebbit Copse. This was established by the Devon Tree Bank and the idea behind it has been to encourage families to plant a native broadleaf as a memorial or for some other personal reason. This, also, is at a point where there is access for all.

The Forest Classroom

A classroom has been provided at Buller's Hill, close to the new forestry headquarters, to enable thousands of Devon schoolchildren to visit Haldon for an invaluable glimpse at what forests are all about. Having seen the joy that pupils have at visiting Haldon it's safe to say that such a utility will enhance these children's knowledge, appreciation and enthusiasm for wildlife. Ask any of the multitude of youngsters, in years to come, whether they remember their school day spent on these hills and the answer will, in all probability, be voiced strongly in the affirmative!

TV presenter Juliet Morris with Phil Chambers and an 'old deer' in the classroom

Haldon's Wildlife

Traffic signs on all the approach roads to Haldon attempt to warn motorists about the presence of deer within the dense woodlands. Many motorists travel these thoroughfares daily without seeing a solitary fallow deer and possibly they may scoff at such signs but they cannot argue with the validity of them. Each year an average of ten to twelve deer are killed in road accidents on the Haldons. To reduce this mortality rate, deer reflector posts have been located along stretches most likely to cause such accidents. Originally tried in the New Forest, there is sufficient evidence to suggest that they are working to reduce the accident rate. Deer reflector posts pick up a headlight beam and thrust it into the wood. The best way to note their effect is to watch by night from within the forest as cars approach. Speculation has arisen about the population of fallow deer within the forests. Attempts are made to keep the resident herd at about one hundred and twenty in

strength. This means that about forty are culled each year by skilled Rangers using high velocity rifles. The male/female ratio is carefully maintained with injured, poorly formed and older deer prime targets. The problem in trying to make an accurate census is compounded by the density of the forests and the extent to which they roam. The Haldons are a much larger area than many people realise. It is thought that originally the deer escaped from local deer parks such as Powderham beside the Exe Estuary. Since acquiring their freedom the herd have adapted most successfully to the Haldon environment. Consequently their colouration has changed visibly with the standard spotted fallow deer giving way to a duller, less marked, Haldon model. Roe deer exist in smaller but increasing numbers especially towards the Teign Valley area of the Haldons.

Robin Khan is a name synonymous with the wildlife of the Haldon Hills. For several years he worked for the Forestry Commission in the capacity of warden. His speciality is wildlife, spending many of the long winter evenings acting as a freelance wildlife lecturer. Without his help, support and guidance, this particular section of the book would be far less illustrated or detailed. I am indebted to him for opening my eyes to the great potential of these forests. Given favourable conditions, and in some cases a great deal of luck, the following creatures have all been seen on Haldon in recent years. Some are common whilst others are less prolific: badger, fox, stoat, mink, short-tailed vole, bank vole, long-tailed field mouse, pipistrelle bat, longeared bat, rabbit, hare, grey squirrel, dormouse, common shrew, water shrew, fallow deer, roe deer and muntjac deer.

To give consideration to more than a few species is impossible. Badgers, so much in the news in recent years, are common on Haldon seeming to favour the Greensand as it gives them a habitat where the drainage is good. They are popular with foresters as they are harmless.

By contrast the grey squirrel is the bane of the Forestry Commission causing massive damage especially in April, May and June. It seems they have a fondness for young broadleaf trees, sycamore and beech being particularly appealing. They strip the bark from these trees, often ruining a potentially good crop. Many smaller birds have their eggs stolen or young removed by these rodents. Many people bemoan that the tail bounty on grey squirrels has been discontinued as it was felt that this helped to restrict their numbers. The short-tailed vole is a tasty little fellow, or so adders seem to think, as without doubt they enjoy eating them. Therefore, an area populated

with short-tailed voles will have an equally high number of snakes. Many people are alarmed by the presence of adders. Robin Khan caught and marked more than five hundred on Haldon. However, he would be the first to reassure people, put off by the thought, that the threat of being bitten is remote. No cases have been reported on Haldon in recent years. Dogs are more likely to be bitten because they have a habit of passing through the undergrowth with their noses buried deep enough to become targets. Even so, such a situation is most unlikely.

Haldon's bird population is healthy with a great variety of species to be observed. The resident birds include willow tit, blue tit, coal tit, marsh tit, great tit, long-tailed tit, yellowhammer, linnet, siskin, redpoll, crossbill, chaffinch, bullfinch, greenfinch, robin, dunnock, wren, goldcrest, treecreeper, nuthatch, grey wagtail, pied wagtail, stonechat, meadow pipit, blackbird, song thrush, mistle thrush, green woodpecker, greater spotted woodpecker, jay, magpie, carrion crow, raven and woodpigeon.

The birds of prey found on Haldon include the common buzzard (18-20 pairs), sparrowhawk (8-10 pairs), kestrel and tawny owl. Others that have been studied in these hills include honey buzzards, goshawks, hobbies, peregrines, red kites and osprey. There is a dedicated vantage point to spy these birds. The 'Bird of Prey' viewpoint is located on the same side of the road as the Buller's Hill car park but about half a mile closer to Lawrence Tower. The location, grid reference SX 877 855, is accessible for wheel-chair users, a short path, cut through a flinty surface, taking visitors to a superb view, apart from the occasional pylon, of the countryside and moors to the west. From here it's possible to appreciate the variety of trees across the hillsides that drop steeply away. On the far horizons some of Dartmoor's better-known tors can be seen, Haytor Rocks being a clearly recognisable landmark. In between is the giant depression of the Teign Valley, an area that is sometimes overlooked by walkers who head straight for the Dartmoor hills. If only they knew what they were missing! High on the east-facing Teign Valley slopes are a number

of villages. Hennock, which seems to hog the contour, is visible down the valley whilst the lovely, scattered village of Christow is almost straight ahead, just to the right of Canonteign House. Bridford, set even higher in the hills, lies to the right. Down below, the church tower of St Michael's at Doddiscombsleigh, is just visible. The information board reveals all about the birds that might be seen in the right conditions so go and have a look for yourself! If you are a teacher intending to take a party

of children or students, if they are physically bigger, then the Forest Ranger should be contacted first at the Buller's Hill office.

Breeding summer visitors, to the Haldon Hills, boost the summer population and include the chiff-chaff, willow warbler, blackcap, garden warbler, common white-throat, grasshopper warbler, wood warbler, spotted flycatcher, tree pipit, nightjar, turtle dove, common redstart and cuckoo. The cuckoo favours meadow pipits for adoption purposes. Many of these species are found within the deciduous or mixed woodland, close to streams or in the denser vegetation habitats beneath power lines. The coniferous plantations do not provide such suitable habitats except for species

like the sparrowhawk or crossbill. The latter likes dry heath conditions, nesting in mature Scots Pine. Larch cones and Scots Pine cones provide part of a crossbill's diet.

A species in general decline is the nightjar which continues to thrive on Haldon. In 1981 thirty-five pairs were noted. It faces little danger in Britain but on its winter migration to Central Africa it suffers from heavy chemical spraying of DDT which is used in massive amounts to counteract other menaces. The lines of pylons that cross the Haldons are veritable 'Jekyll and Hyde' landmarks. Earlier in this book it was observed what disastrous consequences it heralded for the Toyne family. As a direct contrast Robin Khan has made many studies of their influence on wildlife and habitat. His observations are more sophisticated than can be countenanced here but the overall impression is that the vegetation cover beneath the pylons, if carefully managed, provides a most important habitat.

Butterflies thrive in such a situation with thirty-five species identifiable. Only Ashclyst Forest, east of the Exe, can boast more, in the South West area, with thirty-six species.

There are not many natural ponds in the Haldon Hills but old clay workings, specially constructed ponds and the small lakes of nearby country houses help to support a great variety of dragonflies and damsel flies. The fourteen species of

A group of youngsters learning about the forest environment

dragonfly spotted are half the number of species found in South West England.

To analyse individual creatures is interesting but the overall cycle is the crucial factor. So many species are inter-dependent on others and there are many examples; here is but a simple one. If clean water conditions in the ponds are maintained, an increased food supply is engendered for amphibians, for example, frogs and newts. As the amphibian population rises accordingly so does the number of grass snakes as they are exceedingly partial to frogs and newts.

Other forest pests include the vole and woodmouse who cause severe damage to young trees and plants. There are plenty of these creatures owing to their constant and vast reproductive rate. Nature takes its course preventing a population explosion amongst small mammals by providing a wide variety of predatory creatures to perform natural selection.

The Forest of Haldon has plenty of wildlife on view with plenty of privacy available to study the birds and animals without coachloads of devotees of the 'Hudsonian Godwit' ready to trample any habitat into oblivion for the sake of witnessing a natural history freak occurrence. The quiet success of the woods is typified by birds such as the song thrush which have disappeared from gardens in local towns and villages but can be observed frequently on Haldon's south facing slopes.

The forest trails provide excellent access to all the various habitats. Contrary to belief, even on the busiest of days, the twists and turns of the paths can 'lose' hundreds of wildlife enthusiasts, retaining the intimacy and privilege of studying the flora and fauna without disturbance. It merely shows that a carefully managed forest can satisfy the needs of its inhabitants and its visitors.

The working wood with its controlled felling and replanting programme creates secure nesting habitats. Endangered species like the nightjar and woodlark thrive on the Haldons. All we have to do now is to educate more people about wildlife and its relevance. The people who work for the Forestry Commission are not just tree experts but have an immense knowledge and affection for wildlife (except, of course, for grey squirrels!).

THE WORKING HILLS

A lthough you could probably drive around the Haldon Hills for miles without seeing anybody involved in the workaday task of earning a living, it is, nevertheless, a place where many people work. Most of the escarpment is covered in forest so it's probably a case of not being able to see the foresters for the trees!

Geology, Mining and Quarrying

The geological structure of Haldon dictates the shape of the land and the way in which it is used. It may appear dull to some people, but a book of this type, without Haldon's geology, is like a map without a key.

Geologists are a strange breed, being at their communicative best when they are beside an outcrop of bare rock. At such points they eulogise and become ecstatic when evaluating the rock type and its potential origin or usefulness. In the Haldon Hills locations where such outcrops occur are in steep valleys, gorges, quarries and beside tracks and roads where the routeway has either been hewn or hollowed out of the hillside.

Geology lecturers seem to prefer roadside locations, getting so enthusiastic about the rocks that they fail to realise that their students cannot hear them! Deryck Laming had few such problems having progressed to a career demanding immense geological skills. I am most grateful to him for his guidance in an area which shows up my 'faults' so strikingly.

Two geological formations make up Haldon – the Upper Greensand and the New Red Sandstone. The latter is certainly red, and is clear in the soils of the hillslopes and the cliffs of the sea coast, but the 'green' in the Greensand is almost invisible

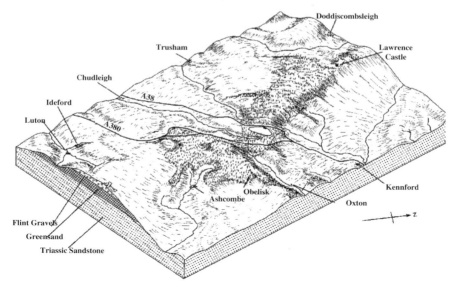

except to a geologist. It is caused by little mineral grains of glauconite, which is dark green and occurs speckled in the sands and sandstones of the Greensand, most of which are yellow or brown in colour.

Chert, a silica rock like flint, is found as large lumps or beds in many places, e.g. Buller's Hill Quarry (SX 883 846).

It is the layer of Greensand that is the reason why the hills are there at all. Like the Blackdown Hills in East Devon, the capping of resistant sandstone and chert has protected the underlying rocks from erosion. The layer was once much more extensive, and lay near to sea level, but rivers flowing off Dartmoor and from mid-Devon deepened their valleys as the land rose and severed the Haldons from Dartmoor to the west and the Blackdown Hills to the east.

Before this happened though, beds of flint gravel were deposited, the flints coming from a layer of chalk that once extended over the area. Chalk is to be found not much nearer than Branscombe, in East Devon, but the flints are clear evidence that it covered the Haldons. There is indisputable evidence that a tropical desert held sway in Devon some 200 million years ago. In the Permian Period the English Channel was a dry desert basin which extended from France to the English Midlands and the North Sea; to the west lay a range of mountains, the eroded remnants of which form Dartmoor and Cornwall. Material worn away from the mountains was carried by rare but violent floods down watercourses that were nearly always dry, and layer by layer the red sandstones were built up.

In the dry times, winds blew loose sand into dunes. These can be seen today in the cliffs around Dawlish, protected from the hammering of geology students by the railway line. The largest dune was over 60 feet high and is preserved in the cliff behind Coryton's Cove, Dawlish (SX 961 760).

The rocks that formed the mountains to the west of Haldon in the Permian Period were, of course, much older, and included the Dartmoor Granite. Near Chudleigh, the limestone outcrops are Devonian in age, but along the western edge of the Haldons the rocks are Carboniferous shales, sandstones and cherts. Igneous intrusions are present in these rocks, notably dolerite which is quarried for crushed stone aggregate at Trusham.

The Ice Ages brought no huge glaciers to Devon – but the weather must have been very cold just the same! Within the last million years three or more periods of Arctic weather have affected the region; the forests died and only tundra vegetation survived. Severe frosts and deep snow drifts caused accelerated erosion of the hill slopes, and it was during those times that the deep combes on Haldon's flanks were probably cut to their present-day shape. George Pycroft (see later details) the nineteenth century geologist, who thought glaciation had a part to play in the formation of Haldon, was not entirely wrong for on the northeast slopes near Mamhead especially, there are dark tongues of bouldery soil reaching down from the top that can only have been formed under Arctic conditions.

The geological section shown reveals the variety of rocks around and about the Haldons. Many of these have been worked in the past and some of them still are.

The dense forests which clothe the upper slopes of the Haldons hide a mass of disused mines and quarries. Mention has already been made of the limekilns for Harcombe Quarry which became the country seat of its resident 'Earl'. In the past Harcombe Quarry worked Devonian Limestone for construction of walls, pavements and buildings for Chudleigh and the surrounding area. These are the oldest rocks in the district, having been formed some 380 million years ago. Grealy Pit near Chudleigh still extracts these limestones.

The Teign Valley area was once a mining district of considerable local importance extracting copper, iron, lead, manganese and other minerals. At Doddiscombsleigh old maps show four manganese mines and a limestone quarry. Old records show that the mines had greatly fluctuating fortunes depending on the price they could acquire for their minerals. Whatever the situation the miners and their families experienced a hard life above and below ground

The purple rock of School Wood Quarry near Dunchideock was formed from volcanoes active some 280 million years ago, at the beginning of the Permian Period. The quarries were worked intensively until the inter-War years but only sporadically since they are now becoming overgrown, with one of the quarries fenced off to prevent rubbish from being deposited. Several local buildings, including St Michael's

at Dunchideock, have been constructed from these Permian lavas. These volcanic eruptions are not locally unique as other examples occur at Killerton, Ashclyst, Ide and at Rougemont Castle in Exeter. The cross-section shows the marked change in dip between the Permian and the Greensand strata.

Another quarry that appears to have 'bitten the dust' for the time being is the flint quarry on top of the Haldon ridge. When operating it was one of the smallest working quarries in Devon and was found on Deers Hill. Most of the year it was worked by two men, but an occasional extra hand was taken on if the situation demanded. Over large parts of the Haldon hilltop flints are found embedded in siliceous clay layers between six and eight feet thick. Despite being a small operation the winning of the flints was an impressive spectacle although out of character with the woodland surroundings. Visiting the quarry, when it was a working pit, meant leaving a roadside scented with the smell of a million pine trees only to discover clouds of acrid smoke. The scene of contrasting industry was tinged with an almost science-fiction feel about it. Smouldering in neat little heaps the calcined flints glowed dully, emitting smoke which made the black and white photos I took that day appeared as if they were over-exposed. The flints were separated from the clay by screening in dry weather as in damp conditions clay is an impossible medium with which to work. Firelighters ignite the mounds of flints to temperatures ranging between $800°-1000°C$.

By doing this, the hard flints were softened sufficiently for them to be more readily crushed and ground. A short lorry journey then carried the finished product down the A38 to the Candy Tile Factory at Heathfield. The flints provided forty percent of the composition of the tile body. Therefore, there is a possibility that you might even have a little bit of Haldon in your bathroom or kitchen!

The Treacle Mines

Three million years ago moss-like plants and sugar cane existed in this area. Through the ages these became compressed to form the treacle beds which exist today. In Devon there are three districts where treacle quarries or mines are to be found. These are at Daccombe near Newton Abbot, Tamerton Foliot in Plymouth and lastly in the Dunchideock district. Fortunately it is the latter which is the most famous and prolific. The two main sources in the Dunchideock area are in the quarries above the village at School Wood and beneath Dunchideock House. Being particularly interested in industrial archaeology, I contacted Mr Archibald N. Winckworth to arrange a visit to the treacle mines beneath his Dunchideock House home. We

descended into the mine at midday one Sunday. Production was at a standstill as the miners had a well-earned day off but evidence of their labours could be seen as barrels of treacle, sold in measures called 'watkins', were located in the corners of the mine. Various items of machinery and implements were left around ready for the next shift to begin or go 'on core' without delay.

Production figures for Devon Treacle is difficult to obtain as the majority of this gourmet brew is exported notably to the USA. In Cambridge, Massachusetts, a 'Circle of Treacle Tasters' has been formed consuming quite a considerable amount of Dunchideock Treacle.

A television company has filmed the mine as

some people have been known to doubt its very existence. To allay these doubts the treacle mine is open to the public once every two years when a fête takes place in the grounds of Dunchideock House. A small entrance fee is charged which goes to charity. Fresh treacle can be purchased, which is most popular.

The processing of the treacle is simple. It is picked or blasted out, crushed and ground. Vacuum distillation concentrates it, producing a heavy liquor. Sealed within wooden vats it matures within ten years. Each batch is different in flavour with expert blending necessary to produce a smooth taste.

The earliest mining is thought to have existed since 1550 when a family called Pitman owned the house. This name originates from people who worked in pits.

Mr Winckworth, mine owner, has received many strange requests. One tourist operator wanted to organise visits for parties on a regular basis. Alas, for insurance purposes the risks were too great and the package to the treacle mines was impracticable: treacle, when freshly mined, is highly explosive. Mr Winckworth would not want anyone to come to a 'sticky' end.

For people not prepared to swallow this story, the treacle also has medicinal uses which can be verified. If bitten by an adder, an unlikely event, treacle can be applied externally to the bite. As a remedy this compound is highly rated.

In an article written in 1923 it stated that in the reign of George IV an Act was passed for the regulation of parish apprentices to provide Poor Law children, of both sexes, from the age of nine with a lifestyle that gave them meat, drink, apparel, lodging, washing, and all the other things necessary for them to reach the age of 21 in a fit state. It's believed that a farmer at Dunchideock kept a number of these farm apprentices to do the bulk of his work. In order to feed them as cheaply as he could he devised a diet that was largely comprised of bread and treacle. He would make regular trips into Exeter to visit the grocers or chemists who sold this on draught. With his cloam pitchers filled he would return to the Haldon Hills in the knowledge that this would fuel his workforce in an economical way. Perhaps the seemingly, never-ending supply of treacle led to the treacle mines myth...

Archie Winckworth

Talking with Mr Winckworth was a revelation, as he knows and loves the Devon environment. He was full of tales about the Dunchideock area. Notably, he told me of a deaf organist resident at Dunchideock church for some sixty-seven years. Through over-use this man had his fingers bandaged in pairs which meant that the sound produced would often be made with two notes rather than one. Being deaf he could not ascertain when the vicar had finished his sermon and therefore would continue with the music when he felt the vicar should have finished. This led to frequent interruptions of the service. At odd times the deaf organist would whisper so loudly to the boy pumping the organ that all the congregation would clearly hear it. Sometimes this encouragement to the pump lad was somewhat secular!

A Geological Adventure

In 1872 George Pycroft, an enthusiastic Victorian geologist, set off on a safari up a river valley of great interest to him. It was not to be the Amazon or the Nile, but Dawlish Water issuing from a series of springs high up on Haldon. His attitude was no different to those who pursued more illustrious waters. He was out to prove that glacial activity once occurred in this valley.

He described the stream as being about four feet wide, six miles long and in some places deep enough to allow a duck to float without touching the bottom.

Visitors and residents would probably disagree with Mr Pycroft's scant dismissal of the last mile of the stream as insignificant, being artificially dammed and landscaped to set off 'The Lawn' and make an attractive setting. Pycroft noted that the stream was so unimportant that it did not possess an official name. Today the map labels it 'Dawlish Water' but like all popular things it has attracted the locally fond title of 'The Brook'.

Dawlish Water has five main sources. The main tributary starts at Grammarcombe near the A380 Exeter/Torbay Road. Others start at Lidwell Chapel remains, Little Haldon, Westley Manor and Higher Charlwood Farm.

The sources all share the same geological beginnings, the junction of the permeable Upper Greensand and the denser New Red Sandstone. Our poor friend suffered in his attempts to prove his case. Spare a thought as he expresses his efforts as:

"From the bridge near the church to the river's source at Grammarcombe the exploration of the river is most difficult, it being so full of brambles and covered in by trees; indeed there is no way of seeing it except by walking in the water. Frequently I was reduced to crawling on my hands to enable me to progress at all. At one point I almost gave up further travel in despair, when I was encouraged by finding a block of porphyritic trap lying across the stream of unusual magnitude."

The dedication and perseverance of this Victorian geologist is impressive. How many of us today would go through such an ordeal taking such consolation from a lump of rock? He makes a few interesting observations. He claims that concealed, buried or hidden in this valley are so many outcrops or near outcrops of rock that if they were all exposed the scene would be as impressive a rocky vale as

Ashcombe Church

Lustleigh Cleave. His theory postulated that these blocks or erratics were transported in an ice sheet as no other transporting agent was conceivable.

In July 1876 at Ashburton, Thomas Andrew read a paper about Dawlish floods. Within this he dismissed Pycroft's theory, claiming water as the agent of transportation after disintegration of the beds on which they lay.

Not wishing to confuse you, a real bed was disintegrated in a flood along the Vale of Dawlish which also washed away a house in Dawlish. On 19 October 1875 the heaviest rainfall in living memory fell in a storm covering most of England. Near Dawlish $3^1/_4$ inches of rainfall fell in three hours which was more than ten percent of the annual expected average. Damage was extensive as, near the Manor Gardens, the force of the water removed several tons of shingle and mud depositing it in the vicinity of 'The Lawn'. This scouring of the stream bed deepened a length of over a hundred yards to a depth of several feet. It was phenomena like this which reinforced Andrew's belief that water was a force capable of removing great weights. Earlier in 1810 a hayrick was carried unceremoniously down 'The Brook' and out into the English Channel. Days later it was washed up onto the beach at Babbacombe still intact. Spectators would no doubt reflect on this uncanny happening – such is the harvest of the sea!

This valley is not noted for its high amount of precipitation but more so for its mildness. It is sheltered by both Little and Great Haldon as well as its own steep sides. Many past meteorological statisticians noted that this was a valley hardly touched by winter's icy hand. Statistics show its mildness, whereas market gardens and arable farms exploit nature's gentleness in the combe. The New Red Sandstone soil of great fertility is invaluable to this industry.

A road from Ashcombe follows this valley all the way to the sea at Dawlish. It is a narrow, sometimes tortuous, road which shows the beauty and warmth of this lovely and almost forgotten Devon valley.

Exeter Forest – a Working Forest

The forests of Haldon have been given a passing mention in many topics already explored. This time they get their deserved individual appreciation as they are the dominant feature of the upland Haldon landscape.

After the Enclosures Act, 1813, had deprived commoners of their grazing rights, the large landowners began to clothe these hills with woodlands. It was a time when large estates like Whiteway, Lindridge, Mamhead, Trehill, Oxton, Haldon House and several others employed landscape 'masters' such as Capability Brown to add extra beauty to their parklands. As a consequence new species of trees were brought in like Evergreen Oak, Sweet Chestnut, Spruce and many species of fir. These supplemented the indigenous trees of ash, oak and beech already well established.

Into this century the estates could not manage their former high standards. In June 1920 Kidden's Plantation was the first to be leased by the Forestry Commission. Over the years they moved southwards, buying leases towards Mamhead before moving northwards and then eastwards to take in even more land and subsequent plantations.

The geology of specific areas is significant for the type of tree planted. The gravel-surfaced hilltops lack nutrients and are best covered by pines. On slopes where better soils are found and the drainage is good, Douglas Fir does well but, if the drainage is impeded, Spruces predominate. There is nothing random about a well managed wood and the variety of tree types found is considerable.

These trees are at various stages of development. Those planted in 1920 are now mature trees with some of these splendid Douglas Firs more than a hundred feet tall. Some of the men who planted them feel immense pride and satisfaction. The work of a forester must be most appealing as Reg Short (Senior), Peter Verney, Henry Tucker, Ron Warren, George Payne and Vic Glass all managed at least 40 years of continuous service in forestry or kindred pursuits. Immense changes have taken place in tree management since those pioneer days earlier this century.

A prime consideration when felling trees is that the Haldon Hills are on view for considerable distances. In order to enhance the scenery a deliberate policy is made not to fell in straight lines or produce hard edges to the tree line. People fail to realise what lengths the Forestry Commission go to in an attempt to create the best environment for what is a commercial enterprise, a working forest.

For many years the various Haldon Plantations came under the name of 'Haldon Forest'. For administrative reasons, 25 years ago, Bovey Forest was amalgamated resulting in the combined name Exeter Forest. From almost every part of the watershed Exeter can be seen, so the name is appropriate.

A forester needs to serve many years to observe the fruits of his work. Larches take 45 years before they are economically mature, Spruces and Firs 50-55 years, whilst Pines take 60-70 years. For those with technical minds 'economic maturity' is defined as the age when maximum annual growth increment starts to fall off. Trees continue to grow beyond these age ranges but become prone to 'windthrow'. To combat this trees develop a root system to resist strong prevailing winds. However, when winds from unusual directions blow hard, particularly after a prolonged spell of wet weather, this natural protection is powerless. This happened in 1977 when an easterly 'blast' caused extensive damage to thousands of trees between Lawrence Castle and Underdown.

The working wood produces timber for many purposes. Saw logs account for 70 percent of production, short logs 10 percent, fencing materials 5 percent, the remainder being pulp wood. Occasionally special needs are met, for example extra long poles for scaffolding, rugby posts and ships' masts.

The Forestry Commission have undergone, and continue to undergo, great change to their working practices. Today their role is one of multi-objective management, trying to please as many people, and creatures

both great and small, as possible in the way their forests are managed. The felling pattern for trees is carefully managed in a cyclic programme to meet the woodland requirements of a vast range of species, in particular the population of raptors (birds of prey), of nightjars and of the wide variety of butterflies. In such a cycle of controlled and planned felling it is also possible to pay special attention to the restoration of heathland, roadside verges and mature woodland. This Management Plan is one that has been agreed with English Nature. As visitors to this hill range will discover, many recreational facilities for bird watchers, horse riders and walkers have been established.

This forest, which has a mixture of coniferous forest and broad-leaved woodlands, has been given the distinction of being the first man-made Site of Special Scientific Interest to be created. This designation applies to some 1100 hectares out a total of 1400 hectares of woods in this vicinity. It looks like the Forest Design Plan is working well at Haldon.

Threats to Haldon

In June 1932 F. J. Widgery wrote a strong letter of protest to the local press, wherein he exclaimed horror at the misuse of the disused flint quarry near Lawrence Castle. This eyesore has since been fenced off and become overgrown. F. J. Widgery had an eye for beautiful countryside as both he and his father were talented landscape artists. His name is perpetuated in an Exeter street name and his initials, FJ, were adopted for vehicles bearing an Exeter registration plate in recognition of his position as Mayor.

The other enemy facing Haldon is fire. On those rare occasions when drought conditions produce tinder-dry undergrowth, a mere flicker of flame can cause immense damage. The loss of the flora and fauna can be severe.

Two examples are quoted, but there have been many heath fires sometimes started by lack of supervision when swaling. This is the practice of burning heathland to encourage a newer and stronger growth in the following season but is not appreciated by fried lizards and grilled snakes! Usually it is a misplaced piece of glass or cigarette end which begins a heathland holocaust.

At the beginning of May 1935 the moorland in the middle of the Devon and Exeter racecourse was set ablaze. Fortunately the race track acted as a fine fire break with no damage to any of the racecourse buildings.

Later in the same decade a massive fire spread across the lands belonging to Lord Mamhead and Major Rayner. The blaze covered an area more than two and a half miles across. Many trees were destroyed, some stumps of which can still be seen like charred memorials. The fire was attended by several fire patrols with the men from the Haldon Ministry of Labour Camp (later Haldon Open Prison) being called away in the middle of a morning service. Although they were successful in 'beating' the fire out, the damage was so extensive that the regeneration process took far longer than anticipated to recreate the forest and heathland landscape.

The Forestry Commission Rangers are especially vigilant in May if dry conditions persist. However, despite the obvious dangers, they are quick to point out that the great majority of people using the forests for leisure purposes are not only responsible but also sufficiently educated to avoid such catastrophes.

If this trend is maintained, the future of these working hills should be secure.

SURROUNDING TOWNS AND VILLAGES

Many settlements are either tucked into folds nestled beneath hills or have clung to the edge of the land where the Haldons reach out to the sea.

Every town and village has a story to tell, some of importance, others obscure. Set out in this final chapter are some of the events, buildings and people which reflect the atmosphere of those places. Those not included in this chapter have, in most cases, already had several mentions.

Chudleigh

Chudleigh is the 'capital' of the Haldon Hills. Small it may be, but if you visit it after roaming the almost totally unsettled hill tops it will assume an altogether more urban importance.

The town is most likely to be entered by the former A38 road (B3344) which has been superseded by a merciful by-pass causing a rebirth in the town's spirits. In the past, by definition before 1974, helicopters would fly over the town photographing the crawling, seemingly endless snake of traffic from beyond Bridgwater and past Chudleigh. The intrusion into the life of this small town was immense. A dated postcard showing the typical sights of Devon depicts surfing in North Devon, ponies on Dartmoor, but streams of traffic through Chudleigh! Such was the trouble and strife which rumbled through its long main street.

Chudleigh now bears some new town signs which proudly forewarn an unknowledgeable visitor that it is an ancient wool town (like many others in Devon) dating back to at least 1309. It has four such signs on its approaches, the cost being borne by Devon County Council and the Chudleigh Amenity Society. The latter has a membership of some 250 which, out of a population of about 3,000, shows a strong community spirit.

The opening of the by-pass has so drastically reduced the traffic flow that it has been possible to stage a carnival again after a gap of several years. One local long-distance lorry driver is so involved with this that he refuses to undertake any long haul, however lucrative, if it would mean missing the event.

The town's name is open to a few interpretations, all of which are Anglo-Saxon, showing that the settlement is about twelve hundred years old. Certain authorities suggest that the first syllable comes from 'cud' meaning a secret, with 'leigh' meaning place. Secret place it may be but 'leighs' are often clearings in a wood. Chud or cud was more than likely a Saxon personal name.

The town has inextricable links with former bishops of Exeter. As long ago as 1080 Bishop Bartholomew built his Palace in Chudleigh. He was Bishop of Exeter from 1161 to 1184. Nearby Palace Farm marks the former site.

The date on the town signs indicates a charter to hold a fair and markets obtained from King Edward II by Bishop Stapledon. Bishop Lacy also did many good deeds for the town and is commemorated by a more secular building 'The Bishop Lacy' public house. This building was once a monks' home being connected to the church by an underground passage. If you look in The Bishop Lacy its doorway is still visible.It is one of many featured in *Haunted Pubs in Devon*.

Chudleigh started to lose its ecclesiastical domination during the Reformation as many of the glebelands were sold to the Duke of Somerset. These lands eventually passed to Anthony Clifford in 1552. The Manor of Chudleigh was bought at a later date by Hugh Clifford from Thomas Hunt of Hams Barton, a farm which still exists about a mile north east of the town. Chudleigh and the Clifford family are synonymous with their impressive Ugbrooke House and Estate to the south east of the town.

It was the wool trade which ensured the town's prosperity. Old records reveal that the town had five mills along the Kate Brook and that such was the extent of the wool trade that a kind of cloth was named after the town. Like all of Devon's wool towns the Industrial Revolution stole the trade with the town decaying in this respect.

As a staging post and market town it remained active despite almost total destruction in the 'Great Fire' of 1807. The compact layout of the town was its downfall as the fire quickly gutted most of the buildings. Just when people felt the fire was losing its force, a barrel of gunpowder ignited. Consequently the damage was so extensive that the town was razed to the ground. As an aside, Bishop Blaize was Patron Saint of the wool trade and not linked with Chudleigh's fire in any other more suspicious context!

The day before the 'Great Fire', a well known local man, John Searle, had died. His body was laid to rest in an undertaker's Chapel of Rest awaiting burial. As the flames spread rapidly through the town his coffin was moved, with haste, into the street, being placed amidst a whole pile of possessions.

Vic Again!

The fire was so fierce that this pile became alight threatening to prematurely cremate the body.

Searle's son left his own burning house in Mill Lane and with help got the coffin to the church. One of the fastest Christian burials ever recorded took place with the phrase 'ashes to ashes' still ringing in Searle Junior's ears as he rushed home to continue his battle with the raging fire.

The fire eventually stopped in Fore Street. When the damage was inspected it was obvious that Chudleigh was almost totally destroyed. A massive campaign followed in an attempt to alleviate the obvious hardship and misery caused by the conflagration. Lord Clifford served the town well by setting up a relief fund and money was raised in a great number of ways, none more so than by his direct influence. After the fire, monies were supplied to those in greatest need for the few weeks following the disaster.

Donations poured in and a general committee was set up to assess need and distribute the money. This was done in a formal manner with every person who sustained losses filling in a claim form. They were asked a host of questions in order to assess the accuracy of their claim, being debarred from claiming on luxury items.

A log showing all the individual claims reveals that Andrew Dodge, a labourer, claimed two shillings and sixpence (12^1/₂p) and got it, whilst William Wright, a maltster claimed £2,583 but only got £1,194. These were the lowest and highest claims respectively. The total amount claimed was £50,694.15s.4d with £42,631.5s.5^1/₂d being paid out in compensatory awards.

In appreciation of the efforts of Lord Clifford, Mill Lane was renamed Clifford Street. Dating houses in the centre of Chudleigh is not too difficult as most of them date from after the 'Great Fire'.

The town continued as a staging post and resting place for travellers between Plymouth and Exeter and remained a thriving market town serving the Haldon Hills, the middle section of the Teign Valley and the Bovey Basin. In 1822 a new coaching route entered Chudleigh from the Exeter direction through Culver Street (now New Exeter Street). This was to eventually become the A38.

One paper that didn't cover the fire was the *South Devon Weekly Express* for it was not established until 1855. It was a special paper for a number of reasons, not least that it was published in Chudleigh for the local populace. It claimed, in its 1950 editions, to be 'The Only Half-Penny One-Man Weekly Newspaper in the World' thus giving Chudleigh people something unique in those days before desk-top publishing made such tasks as this so easy.

The 1950s edition, at only half the pages of the 1930s journal, consisted of a single A3 sheet and carried advertising with British railways promoting 'Summertime Cheap Tickets' from Chudleigh to Newton Abbot, Torquay and Paignton, where the passenger could make the return journey for just a few shillings. There were articles, sports results, death announcements and so on. As it was so personal to Chudleigh folk it went into immense detail of what even journalists would regard as trivial these days. At a fashionable wedding in 1926 when a submarine commander married local girl, Dorothy Mary Cotterill Scholefield, almost a quarter of the newspaper was devoted to covering it. Now this would not be surprising if the page had included a photo or two but it didn't. The names of many of the 150 guests were listed and there was a complete list of the givers and their wedding presents, all neatly done in alpabetical order. The 'happy couple' received a fly fishing box from Colonel Carnegy, a Malacca walking stick from Lieutenant Fleming, three volumes of Johnson, Spenser and Shakespeare from Mr and Mrs Elliott and shooting-seat sticks from Mr and Mrs Herbert Grundtvig.

In a small community it was an invaluable source of information for locals and was very much the effort of Albert Richard Holcombe who printed and published it from his offices in Chudleigh's Fore Street, telephone No. 37!

The present day Chudleigh has a lot to offer visitors. One of its great tourist attractions is 'The Wheel'. It was owned by Hamlin and Whiteway Limited and it nearly burned down in January 1941 when a fire at an adjacent farmhouse threatened to destroy it. Fortunately the abundant water supply, used normally for driving the waterwheel, enabled the Newton Abbot Fire Brigade to douse the fire so thoroughly that major damage was avoided. Papers at the time recorded that the work completed by the Newton firemen was 'first rate'.

Since 1972 The Wheel has enjoyed a rejuvenated existence as a Craft Centre. Its workings have been restored to show how the former corn mill operated. The wheel, with an impressive diameter of 20 feet, was installed in 1860 replacing a smaller preexisting wooden one. This wheel is made from wood and iron with a blacksmith from Ideford involved in its construction. When in operation the wheel managed ten revolutions per minute and the power produced was between 15 and 30 horse power. This mechanical strength was needed as the millstones (Derby Peak and French Buhr) weighed 35 hundredweight each.

Walking around the mill you may observe several names appearing on walls and bins. These were inscribed by the different millers who worked the mill. Another custom of Chudleigh Mill were races up a narrow staircase handicapped by heavy bags of flour on the back. Nothing too unusual you may think, but go and look at that staircase and you will be amazed that such antics were possible.

The Wheel has a range of practising craftsmen and artists that makes a visit worthwhile. Housed within the main building and the outbuildings are many arts and crafts, most of which can be seen in operation producing quality merchandise. To list what you will see is difficult as individuals come and go. Suffice it to say that a visit will be educationally worthwhile as stoneware, pottery, spinning, soft toy making, an old bicycle collection, health foods and a kiddies corner are probable attractions.

The Wheel is beside the Kate Brook at the bottom of Clifford Street. For those interested in industrial archaeology the working parts of the mill are documented by strategically placed cards.

Down the valley from The Wheel are the famous Chudleigh Rocks, caves and waterfall which get a mention in all guide books describing the Chudleigh area. Some famous mountaineers have been known to scale the rocks. The caves are

uncommercialised but their names are more exciting and evocative than the damp, muddy reality suggests. The larger cave contains chambers called The Pixies' Parlour, The Toad's Penance, The Belfry, The Bones Chamber and The Pope's Head. The smaller cave is less romantically named the Cow Cave.

Chudleigh has had a soccer team since 1904. Its most famous result was a 2-1 victory against Torquay United in a Devon Senior Cup match in 1921! Housed at their Kate Brook Ground with views up to the Haldon Hills they enjoy regular support from a number of the townsfolk. Eddie Lee spent over 60 years with the club as an official, a record for the South Devon League. In Chudleigh life Eddie has fulfilled numerous roles from postman to cricket umpire and his public-spiritedness should guarantee him a place in the annals of Chudleigh history. He was extremely helpful in the preparation of *Chudleigh Collection,* which features many fine pictures from the town's past.

Trusham

I know Trusham wasn't included in the original version of this book because several of Trusham's villagers told me so! It's a village somewhat off the beaten track reached through some steep and twisty lanes, which are great for testing the nerve of both drivers and passengers.

Many years ago I was invited to Trusham to give a talk to the WI. So there I was lounging in a hot, soapy bath one cold dark, rainy winter's night when the phone rang to ask me why I hadn't arrived in Trusham an hour earlier! Greased lightning has never moved so quickly and projectors, screens and slides were thrown into my vehicle – but with those lanes the journey from the 'other' side of Exeter still took a good half an hour. I believe the patient ladies have never had such a late talk before but I was invited back so all must have been forgiven and forgotten.

The village, whose name might mean 'village in the wood', doesn't have a shop or a post office but it does have a pub, one that was in the planning stage when this book was first published.

The Cridford Inn in its early days

The Cridford Inn derives its name from a farmer who lived in the pub's building back in 1560. The village had been a 'dry' one for some three score years so the creation of a new inn was greeted with great celebration with almost every Trusham villager turning up to see a procession that was accompanied by the Teignbridge Silver Band. The vicar, the Rev Bill Pears blessed the pub and popular television celebrity, Kenneth McLeod, hoisted the Union Flag outside the inn. This completed a dream for the pub's first owner, Mrs Mountjoy-Gubbin, as for years her friends had told her what a great pub her home would make.

In the *Teign Valley of Yesteryear* there are some pictures of how the village used to look long ago but it's still pretty with many attractive thatched cottages.

According to Arthur Mee, this little village of just under 200 residents, nestled in the valley of the Tame has a war memorial that was lovingly installed: "Just outside the village, below the hills, is a pillared stone set here by 25 men who came back from the war. Some hewed the stone from the quarry, some brought it here, others built it up and cut the inscription, but all made their work a thank-offering for their safe return and a lasting tribute to their comrades who never came back."

The best way to enjoy Trusham is to walk the lanes and paths over the hills and dales in its vicinity and you'll be surprised how close you have to get to the village before you see it.

Ideford

The fact that Ideford has no shops reflects its small size as a settlement but it is the love of small things and underdogs which prompted me to go where few have gone before, in search of human and historic interest stories. After a few enquiries I was directed to Stapley Cottage, the oldest building in the village, to meet Eve who was said to know a lot about Ideford. Stapley Cottage was built by Simon Tapley with money from the 'Feoffee Charities', a named charity which would lynch even the most reluctant victim in a game of hangman or scrabble!

Ideford has lost its village school but not the building. In 1973, through the efforts of the Rev Fred Rawson, funds were raised to convert, extend and modernise the former school, making it a village hall of which to be proud. In honour of the late rector the hall is named 'The Fred Rawson Village Hall'. In order to be of maximum use to the community and to visitors, Devon-style morning coffee, ploughman's lunches and real Devonshire Cream Teas are served. It is possible to purchase local garden produce, preserves and locally made handcrafted gifts, whilst being able to view the work of local artists. The site of the village hall was once the Poor House having been converted in 1836 to a National School. The present building was built in 1856.

The church has existed since 1291 which shows how old the settlement is, probably dating back well beyond Domesday times. The more recent additions to the church buildings have been in stone from 'The Red Quarry' near Ideford Arch. The windows in village churches often create stories of local interest. At St Mary's in Ideford the east window is a memorial to Captain Owen who was killed at Isandhlwana in Zululand in 1879. The chancel side window commemorates the French-Whiteway families as Miss French married Mr Whiteway whose Whiteway estate was massive, clinging to the lower western slopes of Great Haldon.

Quite common these days is the conversion of a pair or row of cottages into one dwelling to meet the expected standards of living space. Two cottages of note in Ideford follow this trend, Stapley Cottage being one and Longbarn Cottage the other. The latter, built probably before the seventeenth century, once saw much of the villagers' dirty linen, and the laundress could often be seen amidst clouds of steam as she toiled all hours of the day.

Ideford is seeing more modern houses built in convenient gaps and on adjacent land. The freedom given by the motor car means that newcomers can enjoy the community spirit of village life, yet have an easy journey to work in the Newton Abbot or Exeter area.

Ideford in the past had two pubs which, for its size, was generous. One, the Royal Oak, has a very special magic conjured up by its hosts. John Pierce arrived in 1973 and it is his personality which has indelibly created an inn like no other.

In many ways the inn should be called The Lord Nelson for within the one-roomed pub there are so many items connected with this famous gentleman. The landlord has immense patriotism illustrated by Union Flags, pictures of national saviours and also many Royal souvenirs. There is even a Silver Jubilee (1977) step leading into the pub.

John Pierce's national pride was triggered off by history lessons at school, 'England Expects' being the motivating force behind this growing collection. John collects and receives all manner of naval offerings which are all housed within the pub. The decor is so unusual that the Royal Oak is like a museum. Lit by candles and a real fire the atmosphere is geared to expect the unusual which frequently happens. Oil paintings of Sir Winston Churchill and Lord Louis Mountbatten preside over the proceedings.

The pub once had a parrot called Walt and at the side of the car park opposite, a diseased elm tree was converted into a totem pole where Walt was buried at the base when he died. In honour of him the top of the pole bore a carved parrot's head. In following years the totem pole was festooned for various celebrations, for example the Silver Jubilee saw it capped by a crown and the following year it flew Nelson's last signal. That was the last time it was fully decorated, on Trafalgar Day 1978. Opposition and various despoiling efforts caused John Pierce to chop it down in

December of that year. Albums of photos kept in the bar, for public inspection, depict it vividly. Each Trafalgar Day many of the locals dress up in appropriate costume having a rare old time at the Royal Oak. On the Last Night of the Proms the landlord transmits the concert into the bar and with fervour, everyone joins in with the sailors hornpipe producing a marvellous scene.

Challenges are often issued to regulars. A typical one prompted them to write a poem on the theme of the pub and its contents. These were read out one evening by the respective poets. The anthology is impressive and again is available for appreciation. Bearing in mind the connection with William of Orange and the Vooghts of nearby Luton, this poem from the collection is a lovely tongue-in-cheek concoction of an historic journey which took place in November 1688.

The Legend of the Ideford Orange Tree

When William of Orange arrived to be King
He came into Brixham by sea
He said to the locals, "You can hang out the flags,
And erect a large statue to Me."
When the statue was up – it was London or bust,
But no excursions were going that day,
So 'His Mob' had to walk – it was jolly hard graft
Via Goodrington Sands and Torbay.
Torquay, they discovered, was closed for half day
There seemed to be no one in sight,
They were all playing Bingo or watching TV
So they tried to make Newton by night.
At Newton the by-pass was closed for repair
And the next train for London had gone,
There wasn't a room at The Queens or The Globe
Then a Police Sergeant moved the lot on.
They covered some miles out of Newton, it's said
When the light was beginning to dim,
Poor old William's ruck-sack was weighing a ton,
With the duty free fags he'd brought in.
Then someone said Ideford was just up the road
And they'd make it for William's sake
But to go any further they'd want double pay
And their corns were beginning to ache.
"We'll stop the night here," William said to his Chief,
"The Old Oak's just down in the dip
I'll mosey on down for a pie and a pint
While you lot find somewhere to kip."
Next day was all hustle and bustle again
To get William's Mob all a-foot
While William was searching the village in vain
To find where a statue'd been put.
But there wasn't a statue in Ideford, alas

All their cash had been spent on the Spree
But some of the lads from The Oak did their best
And stuck up a branch from a tree.
Old William was 'chuffed' when he spotted his tree
Though he wasn't a chap you could spoil,
But he ordered his trumpets to 'sound off a blast'
And decreed they could call The Oak, 'Royal'.
If you should be passing through Ideford today,
Try the Oak for a spot of good cheer,
Take a look at the village where William stopped
In that seventeenth century year.

The oak giving its name to the pub was removed in 1974 and a new oak has been planted in its stead.

One of the Royal Oak's colourful and cherished characters was Terry Jones. His wife, a senior radio broadcaster, interviewed me when the first edition of this book was published and from then on he showed an interest in my subsequent radio broadcasts, down the years, and was more than helpful on a number of occasions pointing me in the right direction for various bits of research. Despite losing much of his sight in his latter years he remained involved with several educational establishments – just one was as Chairman of the Governors of Oaklands School at Dawlish. It was my pleasure to open their summer fête in 1995, and to chat briefly to him and his wife about old times.

Sadly Terry died in September 1995 and many people in the village mourned his passing. Many folk around and about the Haldon Hills will miss his humour, his knowledge and his enthusiasm for so many things and his affection for other people.

The other inn was the Royal George. This closed and became a general store retaining the name 'Royal George Stores'. About 1940, next door to the store, a man strangled his wife and then is reputed to have walked all the way to Chudleigh in bare feet to give himself up. Despite receiving a long sentence he kept in touch with Ideford being keen to know all the village gossip. For a number of reasons the shop closed although with much modern infilling in the village an enterprising entrepreneur might well start a thriving business.

Another village industry which has died out is that of cider making. One farmer especially produced many hogsheads of this potent brew not only for the consumption of Ideford farm workers but also for the many clay workers in the Kingsteignton area.

Luton

This is not the town in Bedfordshire with an airport, but a small hamlet tucked snugly in a beautiful little valley beneath Little Haldon. The settlement was described as "slow, sleepy Luton where the cattle stray indolently about the one narrow street." Citizen's Band radio enthusiasts once code-named Luton as 'Sleepy Town'. This tranquillity was shattered in the years when the nearby Haldon Aerodrome disturbed it with "huge freight and passenger carrying planes that … swoop and soar". Since the aerodrome's closure after the Second World War, Luton has regained its peace. In this period Luton and its valley have shown the results of rural depopulation with several cottages being vacated and eventually demolished. Nearby residents estimate that this small combe has about half the population that it had some 80 years ago. Smaller families and less cottages are evidence of this trend.

A story is told that in 1688 when William of Orange landed at Brixham, he brought with him some physicians, one of whom was called Vooght. This doctor did not reach London because when he saw this little valley he decided to settle in it. The land became effectively his, for services rendered to William. The Vooghts have been at Luton ever since and are still there in force. The lands they tend have been Royal Estates since the reign of Elizabeth I.

Luton was once famed for its flax grown beside the stream but as this industry died out a reputation was made for producing fine quality wheat which was milled on the spot and much of this went to the Newton Abbot area for bread making. The wheat was grown on farms owned by the Vooghts as are the farms called Hamblecombe, Hay and Marsden today.

The building which draws the most visitors in this sheltered vale is undoubtedly 'The Elizabethan Inn'. Parts of the building are over four hundred years old but alcoholic refreshment has only been provided since the middle of the last century when Queen Victoria granted, by Royal Decree, a licence to sell cider and beer. Eventually it became more than a 'cider house' as Heavitree Brewery bought it making it into a tenancy. The pub had been called 'The Albert Inn' since it first opened but on the accession to the throne by Queen Elizabeth II the brewery asked her for permission to change the

name. This granted, it became 'The Elizabethan' as it is known today.

The inn was originally much smaller with alterations and extensions taking place in 1959 and 1962 respectively to enlarge it.

Most inns have amusing anecdotes, and the Elizabethan is no exception. It seems that the pub was run in the 1940s by a couple who caused amusement to their regulars. The pub only had a beer and cider licence which meant that the spirits were locked safely away in the cupboard. This was just as well as the landlord liked 'a drop of the hard stuff'. Occasionally the landlady would fail to lock the cupboard and this would be noticed by the landlord who would consume whisky in large measures. In the bar was a large railway clock that indicated when 'time' was called. Each time the slowly stupefying landlord topped up his glass, the locals would open up the clock and set the hands back five or ten minutes. Consequently on such occasions last orders were artificially extended from ten o'clock to eleven or beyond. Occasionally similar events would happen on a Sunday lunchtime. This time, as well as altering the railway clock, the nimble regulars would help themselves to roast potatoes from the oven.

The present-day inn is well worth a visit if good food is desired in comfortable surroundings at the all-important reasonable rates and these recommendations are made independently after many satisfied visits.

Cofton Creek

Motorists using the A379 road between Dawlish and Exeter will probably be unaware that in some stretches its route once laid beneath the waters of a tidal creek.

Travelling from Cockwood inland towards Dawlish is a level area of land to the south of the road. Various man-made barriers and silting have meant that Cofton Creek no longer stretches a mile inland as it did not so long ago. Near its mouth the remains of limekilns can be seen which converted the limestones, brought around the

coast from Torbay to Brixham, into quick lime for use as fertiliser on local farms. Farmers collecting the lime were keen to use it speedily as quick lime lost its fertility fast. Their enthusiasm frequently led to hot lime on the farmers' wooden carts setting them on fire.

Cofton Creek had three small settlements coming down to the water's edge, Cockwood, Middlewood and Westwood. A bluff or small cliff can be seen along the Cockwood side of the former creek. So that a raised causeway across the upper part of the creek could be created, the land was built up. Above this point the land appears to be a natural hollow. From this crossing point on the creek fine views towards Mamhead Point (the obelisk) are gained. In recent years much draining and reclaiming have taken place in Cockwood Marsh.

On the well drained slopes above Cofton Creek and the Shutterton Brook are those farm lands which geography exam papers delight in portraying as areas of intensive agricultural output. A variety of soft fruit, flowers and other market garden produce comes out of the area from beneath several acres of glasshouses. Evidence of the agricultural pursuits is displayed along this stretch of the A379 with tables of flowers and occasionally soft fruit on sale, market garden centres and the Devon Violets Perfume industry, all prominent.

In the summer months many of the fields sprout crops of 'grockles' (or holidaymakers) and when harvested they yield a favourable return. A sunny growing season is needed for these visitors. The big advantage with 'grockle' farming is that when harvested they transport themselves away in order for a new batch to replace them. This type of intensive farming causes conservationists to become extremely agitated if the crop is too excessive.

Cockwood was one of many Exe Estuary locations used in the making of the cult comedy series *Big Jim and the Figaro Club*. In this photo, taken at Lympstone

harbour, on the opposite side of the river, are members of the cast engaged in filming. From left to right is Norman Rossington, Sylvester McCoy (Dr Who), Gordon Rollings and David John. More pictures and further details are in my book *Made in Devon* about numerous films and television programmes which have been made in this fair county of ours.

Kennford and Kenn

The River Kenn rises to the north of Dunchideock to flow in a general south-eastwards direction to join the Exe Estuary at Powderham. It gives its name to various places along its way, Kennford and Kenn being two of them. Kennford is the larger settlement, a village that grew up along the former main road to

Plymouth. As we have already seen, the building of a by-pass in 1931 helped to preserve the village's tranquillity as motoring to South Devon became popular. The Minister of Transport, Herbert Morrison, opened it in July that year, the road having cost a staggering £23,325, possibly less than the price of a lay-by these days.

Kennford developed along the road and the close-knit nature of the housing made it a prime candidate for some ferocious fires. In the 1920s and '30s alone there were

many serious fires and those in the possession of old picture postcards from either sides of these decades can see how the buildings in the vicinity of the Seven Stars changed in that time.

However the worst fire, in terms of human tragedy, was one deliberately started at the pub called Gissons at the Haldon end of the village.

Clive Biddulph became the new owner on 29 February 1988 but within twenty four hours of arriving there the pub had been set alight and he had been killed. The police knew that this was an arson case for Mr Biddulph's car had also been dowsed in paint

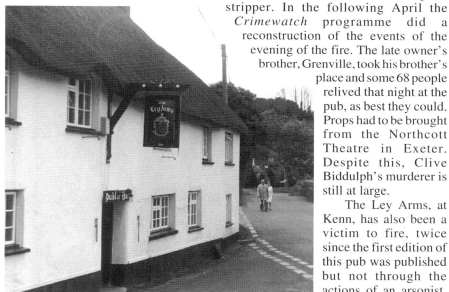

stripper. In the following April the *Crimewatch* programme did a reconstruction of the events of the evening of the fire. The late owner's brother, Grenville, took his brother's place and some 68 people relived that night at the pub, as best they could. Props had to be brought from the Northcott Theatre in Exeter. Despite this, Clive Biddulph's murderer is still at large.

The Ley Arms, at Kenn, has also been a victim to fire, twice since the first edition of this pub was published but not through the actions of an arsonist. In July 1982 the pub was so badly damaged that it was two years before it re-opened only to suffer a similar fate in February 1993.

Kenton

Kenton is a small village about a mile inland from the Exe Estuary, wisely sited above the flood plain of the River Kenn. To imagine that this was once an old river port is difficult as reclamation projects and the building of the railway line along the estuary now prevent the high tides from flooding this finger of the former ria. For the uninitiated, a ria is a drowned river valley caused by a rise in sea level. The Exe saw such a rise in sea level which made valleys like that of Cofton, Shutterton, the Kenn and the Clyst take on a lake-like appearance. Silting, reclaiming and damming have nullified this once potentially visual feature.

Anyhow, moving away from things geographical, Kenton was a port and fell within the jurisdiction of the Port of Exeter. The customs' book for Exeter for the period Easter to Michaelmas 1588 gives details of ships trading across the sea out of Kenton. This log shows that Kenton had five ships listed, which was more than Exmouth or Exeter. Only Topsham with eleven was apparently a busier estuary port.

Some of the ships registered at Kenton were *Nicholas*, *Gregory*, *Mary*, *Trinitie* and *Julian*. They probably worked from other ports with other vessels unloading at the top of 'Powderham Pool'. A register of visiting sea captains is held at Kenton church.

When heavy winter rains and high spring tides swell the Kenn the site of Powderham Pool fills with water to illustrate what the scene must have been like some four hundred years ago. Only the 'Birmingham Navy' would try sailing up to Kenton these days!

Kenton life in the past was dominated largely by the Powderham Castle Estate. The name Powderham is derived from 'Polder' meaning reclaimed land and the villagers were heavily reliant on Powderham for employment. The other two estates that villagers turned to for work were Mamhead House and Oxton House.

In the village were many more shops and activities than there are to be found these days, cobblers, carpenters, butchers, tailors and undertakers being only but a few. It was the lack of communications that resulted in villages being much more self-sufficient in meeting their own needs at the turn of this century.

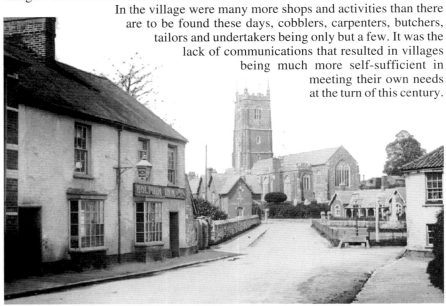

An amusing story is told about one cobbler who made a point of visiting Holy Communion, not solely for the Eucharist but to examine the soles and heels of those kneeling. This way he could decide on who needed repairs or snub those who had gone elsewhere for their repairs or purchases. Another devious trader burned down his shop in order to claim on his insurance policy, in order to sort out some debts. Sadly for him his deception was discovered and he went home to hang himself. At the Victory Hall a musician with a wooden leg gaily tapped out the beat with his peg leg. His actions must have been too vigorous as he went completely through the floor boards. Unscrewing extricated the poor fiddler!

Today the pull of Exeter is great with many of the villagers commuting into the city but, at the very least, they can escape the bustle of city life when they return to their village, a place safely protected from the worst vagaries of the weather by the high and magnificent Haldon Hills.

Haldon Place Names

Names of places can be interpreted sometimes with ease but often with difficulty. The way to tackle the problem of interpretation is to don the hat of the environmental detective and apply logic and guesswork in unison. To this end it is possible to make a reasoned attempt at translation.

A knowledge of the meanings of common prefixes and suffixes is of great assistance. Here is a list to consider prior to examining the actual names:
Barton – corn farm; Ton – a farm; Berry or Bury – an Iron Age fort; Combe – in a valley; Hay – an enclosed or hedged area; Well – a spring of water; Ley or Leigh – clearing in a wood; Don or Dun – on a hill; Stow – a religious or holy place; Ham – a homestead; Ford – a crossing place on stream; Worthy – a farm usually on poor soil.

These are generously interpreted, with purists probably thinking that other variations might well apply. Anyhow, the concept is to understand how or why each name prevails. The parts of the name which may seem difficult to interpret are probably derived from the names of the persons who started the original settlement on that spot. Frequently these characters are lost in time although their names live on being shaped and altered out of recognition.

Trusham – lowest homestead (of the Haldons) or brush wood; Ashcombe – valley of ash; Chudleigh – secret place or clearing in the wood named after 'Chud' or derivative; Luton – Leofwine's farm; Harcombe – hare valley; Cranmers – 'Cranmere' or Heron (Crane) Pool; Ranscombe – Rams valley; Oxencombe – Oxen valley; Waddon – hill where the woad grew; Holcombe – hollow valley; Dunchideock – wooded hill fort; Kenton – farm on the river Kenn; Cofton/Cockwood – takes name from stream meaning 'Red Brook' colour of local soil; Mamhead – teat-shaped hill; Doddiscombsleigh – clearing in the valley, wood named after the Doddis family; Haldon – the hill of hail or holy hill; Larcombe – the valley of the wild iris; Starcross – a cross of this shape but of obscure origin; Ideford – originally Yudaforda (1087) – crossing place; Rixdale – valley of the rushes; Cotley – home in the wood.

By knowing how place names are made up or derived, a lot of geographical or historical knowledge can be detected. Although there are always exceptions to the rule, it is fun to examine a map applying this type of approach.

Some of the stream names can be interpreted. The Kate Brook flowing through the Glen at Chudleigh was originally 'Cranemereslake' meaning Heron Pool streamlet, similar to 'Cranmers' an existing dwelling. The River Kenn is obscure but one loose interpretation is 'brilliant, white'. Most of the district lay within the Teignbridge Hundred, the name 'Teignbridge' continuing into the twentieth century with the District Council.

In Conclusion

Much water has passed under the bridge in the time since I first set out to 'discover' the Haldon Hills but one thing remains the same – Haldon is a place with a past, present and future, a hill range to be enjoyed. I hope *you* enjoyed this look at it!

SOME OTHER BOOKS ABOUT THIS AREA

Pub Walks in and around The Haldon Hills
Brian Carter

Author and artist Brian Carter likes to combine a love of lane and footpath walking with the teasing of the tastebuds – helped by the brewers, distillers, wine and cidermakers. The lane that winds to the Windfall Wine, gales and ales, a pub, pint and pasty pilgrimage with fine old-fashioned Nature Study pave the trail to the bar and the fireside. Luton, Cockwood, Chudleigh, Doddiscombsleigh, Kenton and Dawlish Warren are stepping stones over hills, along the riverside, through coombes and other green places as varied as the weather. The wild-looking farmland around Doddiscombsleigh, the vision of Dartmoor seen from Little Haldon Cross, the Exe Estuary, the tidal Teign, woods, meadows, sand dunes, farm, cottage and stream – in this part of the world you can walk into beauty without going very far.

The Teign Valley of Yesteryear
Chips Barber

This little book is a trip down memory lane to the Teign Valley of Yesteryear through a series of old picture postcards. The Teign Valley Railway and the villages of Gidleigh, Chagford, Drewsteignton, Dunsford, Bridford, Christow, Ashton, Trusham, Hennock and Chudleigh are all featured and for good measure there are some unusual views of Newton Abbot included in this compact collection for your enjoyment.

Dawlish and Dawlish Warren,
Chips Barber

Every town has its characters and stories to tell; Dawlish and Dawlish Warren are no exception. These two settlements with such similar names have very different stories. Dawlish is famous for its black swans, attractive waterfalls and sheltered location, attracting numerous visitors who come back time and time again. Dawlish Warren is like a different world with its more open aspect, sand dunes and ecologically important estuary. It also has an equally interesting and fascinating past. Included in the book are rare photographs of the once thriving settlement at the end of the Warren until 1946, of which there is now no trace.

Around and About Teignmouth and Shaldon
Chips Barber

Which town in Devon once had a shop that sold real aeroplanes? Why did people often wait until 10.30 p.m. to cross Shaldon Bridge? Why did Norman Wisdom, Max Bygraves, Brian Rix and Frank Muir visit Teignmouth? And why did the traffic warden cross the River Teign? Packed with interesting anecdotes and fascinating facts, these and many other questions will be answered in this colourful little book.

Chudleigh Collection

A Chudleigh Collection is a series of wonderful old photographs that show us how things were in and around Chudleigh of yesteryear. Featuring many familiar faces and places, which have inevitably changed as the years roll by, this is a fascinating look at the ancient wool town of Chudleigh. Compiled by the Chudleigh Amenity Society, it provides a stroll down 'memory lane' for everyone – those born here, recently moved here or just visiting for a while.

TV Programmes, Adverts and Films all … Made in Devon
Chips Barber and David FitzGerald

Devon has been used extensively for the making of many films, adverts and television programmes. Made in Devon is a comprehensive and entertaining guide to a vast number of film productions made all over the county. It is packed with amazing behind-the-scenes stories and reveals the tricks of how film makers have turned Devon into the Mediterranean, Tropical Rain Forests, Monte Carlo, Distant Planets, Scotland, West Indian islands, California and many other places. When you read this book you will be amazed at how many famous and well known film stars have visited Devon. This makes Made in Devon an "absolute must" for any film buff or telly addict.

We have over 120 Devon titles; for further details please send a 1st class stamp to Obelisk Publications, 2 Church Hill, Pinhoe, Exeter EX4 9ER or telephone (01392) 468556.